A
HIGHER
THRONE

For David Peterson,
Pastor, Scholar, Leader, Brother,
with deep thanks to God for your time at Oak Hill College

A HIGHER THRONE

EVANGELICALS AND PUBLIC THEOLOGY Edited by Chris Green

Oak Hill Annual School of Theology

APOLLOS (an imprint of Inter-Varsity Press)
Norton Street, Nottingham NG7 3HR, England
Email: ivp@ivpbooks.com
Website: www.ivpbooks.com

First published 2008

British Library Cataloguing in Publication Data
A catalogue record for this book is available from the British Library.

ISBN: 978-1-84474-277-6

Set in Monotype Garamond 11/13pt
Typeset in Great Britain by Servis Filmsetting Ltd, Manchester
Printed and bound in Great Britain by Ashford Colour Press Ltd, Gosport,
Hampshire

*Inter-Varsity Press publishes Christian books that are true to the Bible and that communicate
the gospel, develop discipleship and strengthen the church for its mission in the world.*

*Inter-Varsity Press is closely linked with the Universities and Colleges Christian Fellowship,
a student movement connecting Christian Unions in universities and colleges throughout Great
Britain, and a member movement of the International Fellowship of Evangelical Students.
Website: www.uccf.org.uk.*

CONTENTS

CONTRIBUTORS

Dr Kirsten Birkett is Lecturer in Pastoral Counselling and Youth and Children's Ministry, Oak Hill College, London.

Dr David Field is Lecturer in Christian Doctrine, and Ethics, Oak Hill College, London.

Dr Chris Green is Vice Principal and Lecturer in Ministry Strategy and Perspectives, Leadership, and Homiletics, Oak Hill College, London.

Dr Daniel Strange is Friends of Oak Hill Lecturer in Culture, Religion and Public Theology, Oak Hill College, London.

Dr Garry J. Williams is Lecturer in Church History, and Doctrine, Oak Hill College, London.

INTRODUCTION

Chris Green

Tony Blair's media adviser, Alistair Campbell, once famously announced the boundary line between faith and public life, with the
headline 'We don't do God'. Campbell represented the assumptions
of much of contemporary Britain, where very rarely will any
Christian 'do God' unless they are clergy. Unbelief is permitted, and
even aggressive atheism is given its hour in the sun, but plain,
simple orthodox Christianity rarely breaks cover. Christians, we
might say, don't do public life.

The strangeness of this ought to strike us. Not only is it a matter
of very recent history that atheism has become publicly plausible
as the normal view, and Christianity a fringe world view, and not
only do the constitution, culture and manners of Britain require
a Christian explanation to make any sense at all, but English-speak-
ing evangelicals have noticed and lamented this withdrawal for a
half century, while simultaneously being unable to stop it. The
American scholar Carl Henry published *The Uneasy Conscience of
Modern Fundamentalism* in 1947, but perhaps it was the new winds of
the sixties, seventies and eighties that really brought the clash to
light: the Festival of Light, the writings of Francis Schaeffer and

the foundation of L'Abri, the launch of *Third Way*, the Lausanne movement, the London Institute of Contemporary Christianity and so on are indicators of continuous attempts to form what Harry Blamires famously called 'The Christian Mind'.[1] From one perspective evangelicals have been discussing this for around forty years. But strikingly, that debate has not produced consensus. While it is acceptable to talk about global poverty, HIV/AIDS or the latest Quentin Tarantino film, there is no substantial agreement on them. And even such agreement as there is has made no impact on a culture heading in a very different direction at high speed.

I suspect one reason why our attempts have not succeeded is that the problem is much deeper than we suppose. Theologically it runs deeper because it goes back to sin and idolatry, but that is not quite what I have in mind. I suspect the clues go back through the nineteenth century, through Nietzsche's much-cited but still valid observation that one cannot simultaneously dispose of the Christian God and yet retain Christian morality.[2] His observation

---

1. The situation in the US is, of course, quite different, and it is misleading to transfer terms from one country to another. In particular, the term 'Right-wing evangelicals' is a ludicrously reductionist one, which hardly works in the States, and does not work at all in the UK. Stephen Bates's recent survey of 'The Religious Right' is limited by this blind spot, and therefore not only ignores arguably the two most significant American pastors (Bill Hybels and Rick Warren), but therefore misses their joint stress on combating HIV/AIDS (Bates 2007). It is a convenient shorthand for those who wish to associate British evangelicals with an unpopular American presidency, and in an anti-American culture make us self-evidently guilty and implausible by association.

2. In a discussion on George Eliot, he wrote, 'When one gives up Christian belief one thereby deprives oneself of the *right* to Christian morality. For the latter is absolutely *not* self evident: one must make this clear again and again, in spite of English shallowpates. Christianity is a system, a consistently thought out and *complete* view of things. If one breaks out of it a fundamental idea, the belief in God, one thereby breaks the whole thing to pieces: one has nothing of any consequence in one's hands' (Nietzsche 1968: 69).

was that he saw this happening in England, which means that the sidelining of the theological elements of Christianity vis-à-vis public morality was already well underway by the late nineteenth century. The writings of Karl Marx, T. H. Huxley and George Bernard Shaw made such an impact not because they were radical, but because they were falling on fertile, prepared soil. This then easily moved into the acceptance of the more 'shocking' writings of Oscar Wilde, Lytton Strachey and E. M. Forster.

Where then do we stop in the quest to find the source of the problem? Various scholars have suggested that the decisive change came around that knot of events and thinkers loosely called 'The Enlightenment'.[3] The self-chosen title 'Enlightenment' (*Siècle des Lumières* in French; *Aufklärung* in German) was designed to point up the ignorance of what preceded it, namely orthodox Christianity, both Catholic and Protestant, and its writings could be quite virulent in their hatred.

The acceptability of anti-Christian writings among the educated elite was probably given its most decisive entry point by the publication of two works. Edward Gibbon's elegant and ironic *The History of the Decline and Fall of the Roman Empire*, published in six volumes between 1776 and 1788, the eve of the violence of the French Revolution, is marked by a continual denigration of Christianity and the forging of a bridge between his day and the great days of the Republic; the intervening times were the 'Middle' or 'Dark' Ages.[4] The other work, Shelley's first great poem, *Queen Mab*, published in 1813, was much more libertarian and amoral, and, given what was then happening in the shadow of the guillotine, it is explicitly violent in its bloody demands against Christianity, and against Jesus Christ in particular. But it was written as a

---

3. For a full survey of the way Christians colluded with atheistic rationalism, see Gay 1995 and 1977. More briefly, but no less devastatingly, see Himmelfarb 2004.

4. A similar move had happened two hundred or so years earlier in the self-styled 'Renaissance' (or rebirth) of classical art and culture, but this was not seen as essentially anti-Christian and was usually sponsored by the church.

fantasy, with fairies and castles, and it was designed for the upper-class nursery as well as the study, to arm a generation of children against the claims of the gospel, and to revolt against the Christian God in the name of a greater liberty.[5]

All such literary family trees have deep roots, and one could discover broader connections and longer timelines with ease. But Christians who are thinking about how we engage with public life need to be aware that there is a history to this debate, of both resistance to the gospel and a range of responses to the resistance. Daniel Strange argues in his chapter that the dominant response has been retreat, and colluding in the godless claims of the Enlightenment by conceding ground.

This volume of School of Theology reflects a departure from its predecessors. Rather than deal with a classical doctrine, we are dealing with a rather ill-formed topic, and one where an inconsistent viewpoint has been expressed over time. Even the term 'public theology' is vague. Does that mean politics? The arts? Public policy? Party politics? The answer is probably all of the above, but we do not yet know. This book is not a seamless series of essays but a conversation among people who represent a consistently orthodox evangelicalism, who see public life in regard to the gospel in different ways, but who are committed to thinking biblically on the matter and coming to a common mind. Unlike other books giving a range of views, we hope that by the end, readers will have a clearer view of what public theology is, and how we may use it.

Daniel Strange, who lectures in Public Theology at Oak Hill, has given a summary of the state of the debate, with both historical and contemporary viewpoints.

Kirsten Birkett has a distinguished publishing record as a simplifier and communicator of complex ideas; here she summarizes the thought of probably the most significant but complex of contemporary evangelical writers, Oliver O'Donovan.

David Field takes us back before the Enlightenment, to a great Scottish theologian of the seventeenth century, Samuel Rutherford.

---

5. The parallels with Philip Pullman's *His Dark Materials* trilogy is quite illuminating, and shows how unoriginal the later writer has been.

His masterpiece *Lex, rex*, which later provided a theological basis
for the American Consitution, was condemned in England as trea-
sonable. David also contributes the concluding sermon.

Garry Williams connects the discussion about justice and law to
theories about the cross, and shows how different contemporary
theories about the cross reflect different understandings of how
punishment might rightly operate.

It is a great privilege for us to be able to dedicate this book to
David Peterson, who devised the format for the Annual School of
Theology, and throughout his principalship insisted on the consistent raising of standards of theological education. He has been
passionate about the idea of Public Theology, and it is a delight to
salute him as he expands our vision of a world ruled by Christ,
with 'every nation under heaven' (Acts 2:5).

© Chris Green, 2008

1. EVANGELICAL PUBLIC THEOLOGY: WHAT ON EARTH? WHY ON EARTH? HOW ON EARTH?

Daniel Strange

Our gracious Queen: to keep your Majesty ever mindful of the Law and the Gospel of God as the Rule for the whole life and government of Christian Princes, we present you with this Book, the most valuable thing that this world affords. Here is Wisdom; This is the royal Law; These are the lively Oracles of God.

> (Words of the Moderator of the General Assembly of the Church of Scotland at the Queen's coronation on presenting her with the Bible)

Christianity may have many worthwhile points to make about politics or society, either directly or indirectly, but they are not its main point. Because Christianity does not require a certain form of government, a specific kind of cultural expression, or a distinct way of arranging society, its adherents may legitimately live hyphenated lives that are secular and Christian.

> (Darryl Hart, *A Secular Faith*)

The question remains: how is the church to proclaim the counsel of God as it bears upon civil affairs? It is obvious that there are two means, in particular, of proclaiming the Word of God, namely, the pulpit and the press. The church lives in the world and it lives within the domain of political entities. If it is to be faithful in its commission it must make its voice heard and felt in reference to public questions.

(John Murray, 'The Relation of Church and State')

Introduction

The title of this chapter refers to the 'proud' announcement to friends and family that I had been appointed as Tutor in Culture, Religion and Public Theology at Oak Hill Theological College. Although the terms are notoriously ambiguous, I sensed a flicker of recognition concerning the terms 'culture' and 'religion'. But what about 'public theology'? Blank faces: 'What on earth is that?' was the question. Well, in my articulate way I mumbled, 'It's kind of, you know, Christian engagement in society and public life . . . kind of thing, I think . . .' Blank expressions now turn quizzical: 'Why on earth would you want to teach about that?' Since then, this typical little exchange has become a helpful microcosm, illustrative of a larger bewilderment concerning the state we are in, both the state evangelicals are in concerning 'public theology' and as a result of this, more controversially, the state (of Great Britain) we are in.

This opening chapter has the modest intention of scene-setting for the rest of this collection,[1] orientating our thinking by the drawing of two conceptual maps, the first being a current survey and state of play regarding evangelical public theology in the UK, the second a theological map plotting the key doctrinal coordinates required in locating an evangelical public theology. In other words, I will answer the 'what' and the 'why' questions of evangelical public theology, but in an attempt to move debate forward I want us to add into the mix the 'how' question, presenting for inspection two related yet quite distinct frameworks for evangelical public theology, one, I contend, more satisfactory than the other.

---

1. And of encouraging further reading beyond this collection.

Defining a discipline

What is public theology, or, rather more importantly, what is *evangelical* public theology? Now I do not want us to get mired in defining terms. If theology is hard to define, just think about different senses of the term 'public'. Jonathan Chaplin's definition begins to point us in the right direction: 'The public realm refers to that social space within which individuals and communities or associations interact with each other in ways that transcend their own unique rights and responsibilities' (Chaplin 2004: 5). For the academic *cognoscenti*, 'public theology' is fast becoming a well-established discipline with its own language and grammar, its own doyens, projects and publications.[2] Where better to look for a definition than the editorial of the first edition of the *International Journal of Public Theology*:

> Public theology results from a growing perception of the need for
> theology to interact with public issues in contemporary society . . .
> Public theology is not a new concept, and in fact Christian theology
> always tried to be relevant to its context and society. Public theology has
> emerged as theologians wrestle with the privatization of Christian faith
> and seek to engage in dialogue with those outside church circles on
> various issues, urging Christians to participate in the public domain.
>
> (Kim 2007: 1)

Despite these good intentions, that it is even deemed necessary to call theology 'public' together with the fact that Joe-Public-Christian

---

2. The major centres for public theology within the academy in the UK
   include the Centre for Theology, Religion and Culture at King's College
   London; the Centre for Theology and Public Issues at the University of
   Edinburgh, from which was published Storrar and Morton (2004); and the
   Manchester Centre for Public Theology at Manchester University's Centre
   for Religion and Culture. The Global Network for Public Theology
   (http://www.ctinquiry.org/gnpt/index.htm) was founded at a consultation
   in Edinburgh in Sept. 2005, and from this an affiliated journal was launched
   in 2007, the *International Journal of Public Theology*, published by Brill.

still does not have a clue about public theology says something about
the in-house, isolated, privatized and 'lost' nature of much theology
located within the university. Public theology appears neither to be
in public nor for the public!

However, such isolationism is mutual, for our own ignorance of
the discipline says something about us, because, as usual, we evangelicals seem to be playing a game of catch up. And now as we
wake up and breathlessly arrive late on the scene finally ready for
our turn, we discover that public theology is a game we don't want
to play, indeed *can't* play, because in reality it is a game that others
don't want us to play.

The rules of this game rule us out, for they are the rules of
Enlightenment secularization, which reversed the assumptions on
which theology was historically conceived (and on which evangelical theology always *ought* to have been conceived): theology as
church orientated, praxis-driven 'faith seeking understanding',
built on the unquestioned foundations of biblical inspiration and
revelation, where 'the methods appropriate to theology are dic-
tated by the subject matter and not by objects alien to it' (D'Costa
2004: 188). In what he calls 'Theology's Babylonian Captivity',
D'Costa comments on this reversal:

> The contemporary setting of departments of theology in the secular
> academy has generally institutionally eroded all these assumptions and
> thereby rendered theology into a graceless stumbling knave – far from
> the queen of the sciences. The institutional context is appropriately
> mirrored in a gradual shift of theological method, so that method
> (historical positivism), the subject matter of theology (history, not God's
> action in history) and institutional structure all shore up one another.
> Hans Frei argues that this 'great reversal' ushered in an interpretative
> strategy that stood theology on its head. Rather than 'incorporating the
> world into the biblical story', theology became more and more a 'matter
> of fitting the biblical story into another world' (which was constructed
> by secular modernity and 'policed' by its rules and methodology.
>
> (188)

Ironically therefore, while 'public' theology by its very definition
constitutes a self-conscious attempt to get back to basics, to speak

up and speak out into the church and the world, many of the participants still seem happy to be fostered by the modern university, whose presuppositions are ultimately anti-Christian, what Marsden calls 'established unbelief'.[3] This foster child has taken on some noticeable family features. For example, take David Tracy, in his lecture 'Defending the Public Character of Theology': 'To speak in a public fashion means to speak in a manner that can be disclosive and transformative for any intelligent, reasonable, responsible human being' (Tracy 1981: 350). Alarm bells start ringing here, although this kind of statement is consistent with Tracy's view of theology as a whole. Note this infamous statement in his book *Blessed Rage for Order*:

> In principle the fundamental loyalty of the theologian *qua* theologian is to that morality of scientific knowledge which he shares with his colleagues, the philosophers, historians and social scientists. No more than they, can he allow his own – or his tradition's beliefs to serve as warrant for his arguments. In fact, in all proper theological inquiry, the analysis should be characterised by those same ethical stances of autonomous judgment, critical reflection, and properly sceptical hard-mindedness that characterize analysis in other fields . . . the theologian finds that his basic faith, his fundamental attitude towards reality, is the same faith shared implicitly or explicitly by his secular contemporaries.
>
> (Tracy 1975: 7)

To which I ask, whatever happened to the noetic effects of the fall, and our ultimate commitment that Jesus Christ is Lord?

Alternatively public theology is defined in such a way that there is an inbuilt bias towards ecumenical and interfaith dialogue and cooperation, or where theology is both conflated and confused with the very different discipline of religious studies, the (il)legitimate child of the Enlightenment, and where 'faiths'

---

3. The subtitle of George Marsden's book *The Soul of the American University: From Protestant Establishment to Established Unbelief* (Marsden: 1996).

are assimilated under one genus.[4] To which I ask, whatever happened to the uniqueness, particularity and finality of Jesus Christ?

So is evangelical public theology a contradiction in terms and a dead end? I would argue not, but maybe we need to look elsewhere (and overseas) for inspiration and help. Encouragingly the theme of the 2004 conference of the Federation of European Evangelical Theologians was public theology, the proceedings of which were subsequently published in the *European Journal of Theology*. Again noting the unfamiliarity of the term among evangelicals, editor Mark Elliott describes his discovery as to the meaning of public theology:

> Theology which a) speaks out of the wisdom of the bible and Christian theology and experience about matters to do with public life, matters which touch all citizens, and b) directs itself to be heard by persons and institutions outside of the church. Each of these tasks presents its challenges. a) involves the necessary marshalling of the counsel of biblical theology and the church's collected wisdom on any issue (e.g., 'war') and applying the appropriate hermeneutical 'lens' so that it is a theology suitable for the modern day. b) requires that the church's voice is both understandable by the politician, the voter the civil servant (not in any of the 'languages of Zion'), and that it declares concepts which are to some degree acceptable by those who do not accept the claims of God in Christ.
>
> (Elliott 2005: 3)

Another confessional tradition that uses the term 'public theology' in ways amenable to evangelical sensibilities is the Dutch Reformed tradition, in particular those scholars describing and analysing the polymath Abraham Kuyper, who can rightly be heralded as a public theologian par excellence and whose work and influence has seen something of a revival in recent years:

---

4. For an excellent account of the gradual morphing of theology into religious studies, see D'Costa 2005.

Public theology investigates issues such as the potential for theology to
serve as a form of public discourse and the development and explication
of a theological motivation for public engagement.

(Bacote 2005: 10)

Public theology is not Christian social ethics nor is it political theology,
though politics is a major if not the most significant part of any public
theology. Nonetheless, everything is not politics and politics is not
everything. The word 'public' is of course opposed to 'private' or
'personal' and by 'public theology' I have in mind the careful, theological
thinking about why and how Christians should bear witness in the public
square. Included here are questions about how a believer personally
relates to public institutions, how Christians think about the best way
public order should be constituted, how and to what extent a Christian
should strive to influence public policy . . . it is useful to use the term
'public theology' to indicate those aspects of theological reflection that
are intentionally directed to the interface between the Christian faith and
public life, understood now as the equally intentional efforts of life in the
public civic community, a community shared by many who do not share
our faith.[5]

Having scavenged around for some definitional clarity (and for
fear of now drowning in definitions!), let me attempt my own
working definition: 'Evangelical public theology concerns the theological reflection on the relationship of and responsibilities
between evangelicals and their society / public environment (economic, political and cultural spheres) and their engagement within
that society / public environment.'[6]
Defined like this, I hope confusion can be replaced with clarity,
as all of us see the relevance and importance of public theology
for our lives, our churches and our world. Public theology simply
asks, 'What do the people of God owe to the ungodly? How are

---

5. John Bolt, unpublished lecture, 'North American Evangelical Public
   Theology Today' (transcript given to the author). See also J. Bolt 2001.
6. My definition is itself an adaptation of the definition given by the
   Lutheran Robert Benne, in Benne 1995: 4.

Christians to live out the present in light of the future?' (Tinker
2001: 139). In summary, questions that ask, 'What *on earth*? Why *on
earth*? How *on earth*?'

At this point we begin to understand that what has been labelled
'public theology' covers similar terrain to questions evangelicals
have wrestled with as they try to take the entirety of biblical revelation seriously. As a young Christian I was often confidently told
that the answer to many of my perplexing questions concerning
life and my place in it was that I was to be *'in* the world, but not
of the world'. I was shown substantial biblical support for this statement that I could not deny (e.g. John 17:9–11, 13–19; Rom. 12:2; Jas
4:4; 1 John 2:15–17). However, whenever it came to 'cash value',
I was left hanging as to what such a statement meant in practice,
with the consequence that a wonderful biblical truth started to
become rather trite and cliché ridden. As a slightly older Christian, I
become more and more convinced of the truth of being 'in the
world, but not of the world' but equally more and more convinced
of the profound depth and complexity of such a statement,
needing prayer for God-given wisdom and discernment.

For underlying our seemingly simple statement are huge theological tectonic plates put up against each other. If we start from the
beginning, we see both the goodness of creation ('the earth is the
LORD's and the fullness thereof', Ps. 24:1), but also the 'badness' of
a fallen 'world' ('Do not love the world or the things in the world',
1 John 2:15). Or, from the perspective of praxis, we have to obey
and relate both the cultural mandate to 'fill the earth and subdue it'
(Gen. 1:28) to the gospel mandate to 'make disciples of all nations'
(Matt. 28:19). In terms of God's revelation we have to compare and
contrast our knowledge of him in creation and our knowledge of
him in his revealed Word in Scripture and in Christ. Even if we
choose to start at the end, we have to account for biblical teaching
on both the continuity *and* discontinuity between the earth now, and
the new heaven and new earth to come.

Paradoxically the pinnacle of creation, humankind created in
the image of God, also highlights the pinnacle of the complexity.
First, 'not of the world' believers have to work out how they are to
live among and interact with 'of the world' unbelievers. Second,
Christians have to account that just as they continue to battle with

sin in their hearts, so non-Christians are often producers of great
cultural achievement. Consider the following everyday examples.
Am I wrong not to worry whether the computer I am using to
type this chapter was made by a Christian or not? Am I right to
be concerned when a Christian friend of mine marries a non-
Christian? Am I wrong not to vote in an election because I will be
associating myself with unbelievers voting for the same party? In
trying to influence public policy can I rely on a measure of divine
law and common sense left in natural man 'and that given a proper
choice and good conditions, he may well choose biblical justice
without himself being biblically converted'? (Brown 1989: 253).

Alternatively consider the following biblical examples. The
Israelites 'plundered' the Egyptians (Exod. 12:35–36), and yet Paul
is clear that Christians are not to be unequally yoked (2 Cor. 5:14).
The Samaritans were not allowed to help the people of God in the
rebuilding of the temple, and yet Phoenician workmanship was
welcomed (Ezra. 3 – 4). In Galatians we are told to 'do good to
everyone, and especially to those who are of the household of faith'
(Gal. 6:10). If our first priority is to look after other believers, does
doing 'good to everyone' fully explain the culture-transforming
power of the gospel in the first few hundred years on the church,
which turned the world upside down? Being 'in the world but not
of the world' suddenly seems quite a messy business! What are the
boundary lines that mark out legitimate commonality from an ille-
gitimate compromise, and what are the theological presuppositions
behind our drawing of them?

The story so far

Given the above, my contention is that evangelicals have been
reflecting upon public theology questions for many years, but
without calling it 'public theology'. Two intra-evangelical debates
come most readily to mind: first, evangelical thinking concerning
culture and world view, and second, the infamous 'evangelism versus
social action' debate. Regarding these two hot potatoes, I wish tenta-
tively to suggest that among classical evangelicals there may be
beginning to emerge something approaching a consensus on such

issues, some common ground we can build upon as we construct an evangelical public theology. Here then are some revision notes on the thawing of the evangelical mind.[7]

Evangelicals, culture and world view

Regarding our engagement with culture, there is an acknowledgment that critical cultural engagement in our world is not only unavoidable (for we are all coated in culture[8]) but is biblically mandated. As God's image bearers and vicegerents we have been given dominion over God's creation: the so-called cultural mandate of Genesis 1:28 and 2:15, to fill and subdue, tend and keep. 'God has revealed Himself as a Speaker and a Maker, and thus the immediate significance of being made in His "image" is that Adam and Eve were created to speak and make . . . to be the image of God is to be a creative speaker and producer of "cultural" products . . .' (Leithart 1999: 30).

While being aware of variations on this theme, either by accentuation or diminution,[9] I will not simply examine the reactive task of cultural clashes and deconstruction (e.g. the so-called culture-wars) but also creation and the secondary environments we make for ourselves, and suggest more biblical cultural patterns. However, there is also a recognition that, given the richness of

---

7. I use this phrase in referring to Mark A. Noll's classic study *The Scandal of the Evangelical Mind* (Noll 1994).

8. Here I find William Romanowski's definition helpful: 'Culture refers to the network or system of shared meaning in a society, a conceptual collection of ideals, beliefs and values, ideas and knowledge, attitudes and assumptions about life that is woven together over time and is widely shared among a people. It is a kind of invisible blueprint – a map of reality that people use to interpret their experience and guide their behaviour. The term culture refers directly to this fabric of meaning that is a people's way of life, and in its general usage also describes the "texts" of everyday life and material works that are a manifestation of a cultural system' (Romanowski 1996: 306).

9. For examples of the former, see Hegeman 1999 and Field 2007. For the latter, see Fesko 2007 and Coekin 2006: 33–48.

biblical teaching on culture and cultural engagement together with
the variety of situations in which contemporary Christians find
themselves, placing the evangelical faith exclusively within one of
Richard Niebuhr's *Christ and Culture* categories will be seen to be
both simplistic and reductionistic (this is the subject of Carson
2008).

A complementary truth to the above is our recognition that
engagement with culture is engagement at the level of 'world
view', which James Sire has recently redefined in a more expansive
fashion than in his classic *The Universe Next Door* (now in its 4th
ed.):

> A worldview is a commitment, a fundamental orientation of the heart,
> that can be expressed as a story or in a set of presuppositions
> (assumptions which may be true, partially true or entirely false) which we
> hold (consciously or subconsciously, consistently or inconsistently) about
> the basic constitution of reality, and that provides the foundation on
> which we live and move and have our being.
>
> (Sire 2004a: 122)

Putting these together we discern a relationship between both
culture and world view (culture as world view exteriorized, and
world view as culture interiorized)[10] and between culture, world
view and 'religion'. As Frame notes:

> Culture is what a society has made of God's creation, together with its
> ideals of what it *ought* to make. Or maybe we should put the ideal first.
> People make things, because they already have a plan in view, a purpose,
> a goal, an ideal. The ideal comes first, then making things. First the
> norm, then the cultivation, the culture. So now we can see how culture

---

10. I thank Ted Turnau for this insight in personal correspondence. He help-
fully continues, 'In other words, the specific contours of the products that
we make come from our understanding of the world, our *Weltanschauung*,
and as carriers of worldview, these cultural products (or "texts") contour
our consciousness along the lines of the worldviews they carry.' As we will
see below, the closeness of this relationship is disputed.

is related to religion. When we talk values and ideals, we are talking religion. In the broad sense, a person's religion is what grips his heart most strongly, what motivates him most deeply. It is the value that transcends all other values. So Henry Van Til says that 'culture is simply the service of God in our lives; it is religion externalized.' It is interesting that that Latin term *colere* I mentioned earlier, from which we get the word *culture* also refers to religious service, and comes into English as *cult*, *cultic*, and so on. Culture and cult go together. If a society worships idols, false gods, that worship will govern the culture of that society. If a society worships the true God, that worship will deeply influence, even pervade its culture. If, like ours, a society is religiously divided, then it will reveal a mixture of religious influences.

(Frame 2001: 5)

What must be noted is that biblically speaking, post-fall, humanity is not divided into 'religious' as opposed to 'non-religious' but rather those who have 'true faith' as opposed to what the Reformed Scholastic Francis Turretin calls 'false faith' (Turretin 1992–7, 1: 605 [9.6.9]).

Reflecting on and engaging with culture and world view is seen to be crucial for at least three reasons. First, for our own sanctification and godliness we are to keep ourselves from idols (1 John 5:21), which entails a certain amount of cultural literacy, knowing how idolatrous culture affects us from without and within, not just in so-called religious matters but in all areas of life. Schlossberg comments on those who think they are immune from such thinking:

The emphasis on ideas and beliefs in this discussion does not find warm welcome in an age that respects the tough minded pragmatist who disdains philosophy and insists on the immediate, the concrete and the practical. But it is impossible for anyone to say that he will avoid philosophies and simply live pragmatically, because that statement is based on a philosophical belief that he has accepted without realising it . . . those philosophies may come down in transmogrified form, but come down they do. That is the wisdom of John Maynard Keynes's remark that 'Madmen in authority, who hear voices in the air, are distilling their frenzy from some academic scribble a few years back.'

Our anti-philosophers are especially vulnerable in this age, because
the media fill our environment with popularized philosophies. Marshall
McLuhan was right in saying that environments tend not to be
noticed . . . We do not see the environment, as Os Guinness says
because we see with it. That means we are influenced by ideals we do not
notice and therefore are not aware of their effect on us. Or, if we see the
effect, we find it difficult to discover the cause.

(Schlossberg 1990: 7)

Second, for our evangelism, apologetics and mission we are
required in loving our enemies to understand them, which means
understanding the world views they construct, the cultures they
build, the 'gods' they worship, their anxieties, hopes, plausibility
and implausibility structures.[11] We will take time to do this, all with
the aim of communicating the gospel of Jesus Christ effectively to
them, gently and respectfully debunking their idols, ideologies and
pseudo-gospels (at the individual, familial, societal, political level
etc.), removing their false assurance by showing that their 'gods'
cannot do what is pretended of them, showing them the truth of
the Christian world view and the 'contradictive or subversive
fulfilment'[12] of the gospel, and calling them to repentance and
faith in Jesus Christ.

Third, we recognize that God is to be glorified in everything
we do, that Christ is Lord over every area of life and sphere of
culture, and that Christians have a duty to challenge areas where
this rule is not respected. We must take every thought captive for
Christ (2 Cor. 10:5).

---

11. Sire's definition of plausibility structures is helpful: 'A plausibility structure is a web of beliefs that are so embedded in the hearts and minds of
the bulk of a society that people hold them either unconsciously or so
firmly that they never think to ask if they are true. In short, a plausibility
structure is a worldview of a society, the heart of a community . . . One
of the main functions of a plausibility structure is to provide the background of beliefs that makes arguments easy or hard to accept' (Sire
2004a: 112).

12. Hendrik Kraemer's helpful delineation (Kraemer 1939: 5).

The evangelism versus social action debate

Regarding the seemingly endlessly rehearsed debate over the relationship between evangelism and social action, there is not the space to narrate the history (see Chester 1993): the era of social involvement in the nineteenth and early twentieth century; the 'Great Reversal'[13] between 1910 and the late 1930s as a reaction to the social gospel;[14] the reversal of the Great Reversal typified by Lausanne in 1974, and Lausanne II in 1989, and then the ensuing debate as to whether this great reversal was indeed so 'great', leading some into what might be called a reversal of the reversal of the 'Great reversal'.[15] Again, out of these debates (which have often generated more heat than light), I detect a willingness for peace talks and proper dialogue. Recently a number of evangelicals made important and creative contributions that furthered debate among the classical evangelical constituency in the United Kingdom.

Tim Chester likens the relationship between evangelism and social action to that of a text and its context and summarizes his position in three propositions: (1) evangelism and social action are distinct activities; (2) proclamation is central; (3) evangelism and social action are inseparable (Chester 2004: 64–65). He writes:

> Many evangelicals want to argue that evangelism and social action are equal activities. They describe evangelism and social action as two wings of a bird or the blades of a pair of scissors. While evangelism and social action are partners in many situations, it is inadequate to think of them as corresponding activities of equal impact . . . the greatest need of the poor, as it is for all people, is to be reconciled with God and escape his wrath. Only the message of the gospel can do this. The adage, often

---

13. The title of David Moberg's book *The Great Reversal: Evangelism versus Social Concern* (Moberg 1973).

14. Associated most closely with mainline protestant liberalism especially in the work of Walter Rauschenbusch (1861–1918).

15. Three more negative interpretations of evangelicalism's 'mislaid social conscience' are those of Melvin Tinker (Tinker 2001), Rachel Tingle (Tingle 1995) and John Woodhouse (Woodhouse 1988).

attributed to St Francis of Assisi, 'Preach the gospel, use words if
necessary' will not do. Social action can demonstrate the gospel, but
without the communication of the gospel message, social action is like a
signpost pointing nowhere. Indeed without the message of the gospel it
points in the wrong direction. If we only do good works among people,
then we point to ourselves and our charitable acts. People will think well
of us but not of Jesus Christ. We may even convey the message that
salvation is achieved by good works. Or we may convey the message that
what matters most is economic and social betterment. We must not do
social action without evangelism.[16]

(65)

Similarly American church-planter and evangelist Tim Keller
argues that the ministries of word and deed are both necessary,
inseparable and have a symbiotic relationship, but that 'the ministry
of the word is the more radical and basic of the two ministries, in
that it goes to the root or the fount from which all human broken-
ness flows' (Keller 1989: 116). However, mercy ministry within the
church can lead to conversions, as it creates a plausibility structure
for the gospel, displaying Christian compassion at the community
level (211–212); can build bridges to 'unwebbed' unbelievers who
otherwise would not be reached (212–213); and serves as a communication channel for the gospel:

> Mercy is not simply a 'bridge,' a way to meet people with whom we can
> proclaim the gospel. It actually is a communication of the gospel along
> with our words. It is a visual aid, a nonverbal medium message . . . we
> communicate the gospel most effectively when we are both speaking
> and doing.
>
> (214–215)

In his 'An Evangelical Rationale for Social Action', written for
the Social Issues Committee for the Diocese of Sydney, Michael
Hill writes the following helpful statement:

---

16. Chester has been heavily involved with The Micah Network and the
    model of 'integral mission' they have endorsed (see Chester 2002).

Social action is a necessary part of the Christian life. Becoming a new creature in Christ transforms a person, making them other-person centred and loving. Social action flows from love and is an aspect of doing good to others. Since people are social and relational beings their good is found not only in right personal relationships but in the social structures which frame those relationships. While social action is necessary there is a sense in which evangelism is primary. God's rule and kingdom is not brought about by social action. People enter the kingdom and come under God's rule by hearing and responding to the gospel. Evangelism is primary in a temporal sense. One has to be brought under the explicit rule of God and transformed by the gospel before one becomes a member of the people of God. But once people are brought into the community of believers where God rules they are transformed by the Spirit and the fruits of the Spirit will manifest themselves. The logic of God's domain requires its members to be committed to the good of all people. The relationship of evangelism to social action is analogous to the relationship between the entry point to a structure and the environment within the structure. Entry to God's domain is logically tied up with the shape of God's domain. A commitment to love and social action follows from coming under God's rule. There is no point to entering a right relationship if one is not going to be subject to the demands of that relationship. Evangelism cannot be an end in itself. Evangelism, when it meets a positive response, leads to a right relationship with God and that relationship has to be lived out otherwise there is no point to entering it. Evangelism and social action are like shape and size, you can't have one without the other.

(Hill 2007: 13)

Melvin Tinker, puts forward a 'servant solution' (Tinker 2007) to the relationship between evangelism and social action, concentrating on a detailed exegesis of Matthew 5:13ff. and the metaphors of salt (which he argues as prophetic-word ministry) and light ('God's people are to embody and express the new life of the kingdom amongst themselves and outwards to others' [23]) and a city on a hill ('there can be no retreat *from* the world for these kingdom people if they are to be a light *to* the world' [21]), before looking, first, at how this was applied by the early church in Acts, and second, at the contemporary applications. He concludes:

In his teaching, Jesus presents 'being salt' and 'being light' as two
different, but intrinsic and integrally related, aspects of what it means to
be members of his covenant community. While it may legitimately be
argued that theologically evangelism has priority for the church . . .
operationally, social action, as an expression of the community's 'light',
cannot be neglected without bringing into question the church
community's covenantal integrity, its saltiness.

(31)

Richard Mouw, from within a more tradition-specific Calvinist
community, touches upon public theology issues in his 2000 Stob
lectures on culture and common grace. Arguing from 1 Peter
2:11–17, from which he draws direct parallels back to Jeremiah 29
with its mandate for the exiles to 'Seek the welfare of the city',
Mouw argues for a Christian civility:

The case for Christian civility, as I see it, requires that we establish two
important principles. The first is that Christians must actively work for
the well-being of the larger societies in which we have been
providentially placed. And the second is that sanctified living should
manifest those subjective attitudes and dispositions – those virtues, if
you wish – that will motivate us in our efforts to promote societal health.

(Mouw 2001: 76)

Mouw's theological justification for such Christian activity is an
application of the Reformed doctrine of common grace.[17] He
argues that Christians are to be agents of common grace and to be
engaged in 'common grace ministries': the teaching that God has a
positive, albeit non-salvific, regard for those who are not elect, a
regard that he asks us to cultivate in our own souls (82).

Finally, and arguably the most detailed proposal within the UK
context is that of the Jubilee Centre under the chairmanship of

---

17. In his own exposition of this doctrine, John Murray defines common
grace as 'every favour of whatever kind or degree, falling short of
salvation, which this undeserving and sin-cursed world enjoys at the
hand of God' (J. Murray 1977: 96).

Michael Schluter. The Centre recently produced their most substantial volume to date, *Jubilee Manifesto: A Framework, Agenda and
Strategy for Social Reform* (Schluter and Ashcroft 2005), of which they
write, 'It is not just the fruit of over thirty years of reflection on
biblical teaching relating to political ideologies, but is also the fruit
of over twenty years of active engagement in public life in Britain
and beyond' (18).

Schluter and his fellow-workers see their task as distinct from
but accompanying, complementing and giving credibility to evangelism: '[T]he church as a body of God's people ought to have a
reputation for both attacking what is wrong and actively promoting
what is good, which will make its message credible and attractive to
outsiders' (26). Again this is seen to be a mutually beneficial both–
and relationship:

> The link between being active in putting right the injustice in society and
> national spiritual revival is found often in the prophets, as well as in more
> recent church history . . . Reform seeks to create an environment in which
> it is easier to live righteously. It is both reasonable and right to seek to
> mould a society so as to minimize the conflict between Christ and culture.
>
> (26–27)

What must be noted is the scope and depth of this vision. Building
from biblical foundations, in particular Chris Wright's hermeneutic of the Old Testament,[18] as well as promoting a social/public

---

18. 'Israel was intended to function as a paradigm for others. In my view this
    is not a hermeneutical ruse imposed on the Old Testament retrospectively
    by us, but was part the intentionality of election from the beginning . . .
    Their concrete existence in history functions, not in spite of its particular-
    ity but precisely through and because of it, to disclose the kind of ethical
    behaviour, attitudes and motivation that God requires universally in
    human communities. The reality of this people, rendered to us in the Old
    Testament scriptures, generates an ethic of paradigm and analogy, in
    which we assume the moral consistency of God and ask, "If this is what
    God required of them, what, in our different context, does God require
    of us?" ' (Wright 2005: 81).

paradigm called 'relationalism' (see Schluter and Ashcroft 2005: chs. 2, 6, 15, 16), the Jubilee Centre is concerned with structural social *reform*:

> It is essential to reform the structures of society and influence the terms of debate in order to create a society which sustains relationships and within which Christian service and mission can flourish. This requires moving from fighting limited tactical battles to strategic co-belligerence for the common good. It means real engagement with those who are not disposed to listen to the gospel. Explicitly Christian service and witness are important. The church must let the light of its good deeds shine, and the gospel must be verbally proclaimed. But in many places Christians no longer have (or have never had) a privileged position from which to shape the institutions of society. It is in this context that the biblical vision will also need to be commended as a shared vision. This is not on the basis of the real but not universally acknowledged authority of Christ the Lord, but because it is a demonstrably plausible account of human flourishing.
>
> (31)

Rejecting two alternative constructions

If the above configurations between evangelism and social action are approaching the truth of the matter, I would like to suggest the following implications. First, as *classical* evangelicals we can finally agree with R. K. Johnstone's oft-quoted statement:

> That evangelicals should be involved socially has become a foregone conclusion. . . . but how and what evangelicals are to be involved themselves in society have proven to be more vexing questions. That they are to be involved brings near unanimity; how that involvement takes shape and what is its Christian motivation brings only debate.
>
> (Johnstone 1979: 79)

Second, if this analysis is correct, then I think we are able to steer between two alternative constructions. Often they are the straw men we build ourselves to tear down, but that unfortunately are still, I believe, alive and kicking. However well

intentioned, they are inadequate in differing degrees of serious-
ness.[19]

The first straw man I call 'a diluted gospel': *In our desire for social
transformation, we assume or deny the call for repentance and faith through the
proclamation of the apostolic gospel and so lose our distinctiveness and
effectiveness in public life.* Little need be said here, as in its most acute
form this position resembles, in both theological method and
content, more nineteenth-century Schleiermachian liberalism and
Rauschenbusch's 'social gospel', than classic evangelicalism.

I wish to make more detailed comment on the second straw
man, which I call 'a muted gospel': *In our desire to call for repentance
and faith through the proclamation of the apostolic gospel we forget the power
and relevance of the gospel for social transformation and so lose our place in
public life.*

Here the encroaching epithet is that of 'pietism'. Melvin Tinker
muses on the following illustration:

> One well-known evangelical Bible teacher from Britain was travelling
> with a white church minister in South Africa along a coastal road after
> apartheid had ended. On coming to a particularly attractive stretch of
> beach, the South African pointed to it and said approvingly, 'That used
> to be a "whites only" beach. Now it is open to all.' The response of his
> English visitor was simply to shrug his shoulders and say, 'It doesn't
> matter one way or the other – it is not a gospel issue.' What he meant,
> of course, was that whether people could or could not use that beach
> because of the colour of their skin did not have any direct bearing on
> their eternal destiny: that was to be determined by their response to the
> gospel message. However, from another viewpoint he was profoundly

---

19. Naturally both these categorizations raise the question as to how con-
    sciously or unconsciously, consistently or inconsistently, the gospel has
    to be 'diluted' or 'muted' before becoming 'a different gospel'. Scriptural
    teaching seems clear that such judgments require careful and prayerful
    discernment within a prescribed process, but that such judgments can and
    should be made. However, I wish to use these categories as warning flags
    within which we are able to discuss the most biblically faithful models for
    societal engagement and public theology.

mistaken. It *was* a gospel issue, for not only did such restrictions constitute a barrier to black people in particular from hearing the gospel, especially from whites who introduced such discriminatory laws, but it denied a fundamental tenet of the gospel, namely, that in Christ there is 'neither male nor female, Jew nor Greek, slave nor free'. Here is a failure to recognize that the gospel has certain entailments which need to be worked through that go beyond private morality.[20]

And as Keller notes:

[T]he gospel is the way that anything is renewed and transformed by Christ – whether a heart, a relationship, a church, or a community. It is the key to all doctrine and our view of our lives in this world. Therefore, all our problems come from a lack of orientation to the gospel. Put positively, the gospel transforms our hearts and thinking and approaches to absolutely everything.

(Keller 2007: no p.)

Some are deeply frustrated regarding this mutedness within classic evangelicalism. In a paper entitled 'Why the Reformed Suspicion of Social Action?' Dewi Hughes (Hughes 2001: 24–28) lists seven reasons for such unjustified suspicion, some of which, I would argue, bite more deeply than others. Six of these reasons are as follows:

1. A fear of the Social Gospel.
2. A lack of appreciation of the Reformed doctrine of God.
3. An unbalanced view of Old Testament law.
4. An inadequate doctrine of the gifts of the Spirit or an inadequate ecclesiology.
5. An excuse for worldliness.
6. A result of a lack of direct experience of poverty.

The most interesting reason he gives, though, is what he calls the 'acquiescence in the modernist divorce between sacred and

---

20. In unpublished correspondence with the author.

secular', a dualist view of human beings that fits modernistic thinking well:

> By the middle of the twentieth century any Christian who dared to make a comment about the conduct of public life was very generally shouted down because it had become an assumption that Christianity was a matter of fostering individual spiritual experience that had nothing to do with the way in which the country was governed. I find it very odd that Reformed people who believe in a sovereign God who is the ruler of heaven and earth are happy to accept the position given to them by modernism. To denigrate Christian involvement in society is to accept the place that the world has given us.
>
> (26)

This criticism is stinging and I, for one, wince at it. The issue is not so much a conscious biblically well-thought-through support for a secular state, limited cultural engagement, and modest expectations of success (more of which later). Rather it is that liberal secular humanism has gradually bullied us into a privatized silence and we have not protested, let alone offered constructive alternatives, because we are not interested in such matters. And even if we were, we would not know what to say. It is at this point that we have not kept ourselves from ideological idols, have not taken every thought captive for Christ, have not applied Jesus' lordship to public life. We despair over the state of our nation and yet our unthinking inactivity is partly to blame for the state we are in.

Surveying the current scene

Let us briefly turn our attention away from matters primarily reflective and abstract, to that of concrete praxis 'on the ground'. For while all this necessary reflection and debate has been going on in various quarters, some evangelicals have been getting on with getting involved in society and public life.

What exactly is the state of evangelical societal engagement in 2007, and what are we to make of it? In his *Who Runs This Place? An Anatomy of Britain in the 21st Century* Anthony Sampson deals

with the individuals and institutions that make Britain tick. In the
introduction he writes, 'I do not feel qualified to explain the
churches, whose political influence may well be increasing but is
difficult to assess and analyse' (Sampson 2004: xiii). Regarding the
role of evangelicals in British national life I feel a similar trepida-
tion, being neither primarily a social scientist nor a social
historian.[21] However, I notice that recently there have been signs
of what we might call the 'resurfacing' of evangelical activity
regarding matters of public life. As always it is difficult to speculate
on the reasons behind such a resurfacing, but it may be a mixture
of factors.

First, and already mentioned, factors such as internal theological discoveries and rediscoveries concerning matters of
culture, world view and social engagement. Second, providential
external social conditions have woken us up and forced us to
react: our ever-crumbling Christian heritage, the evangelical crusades of secular humanism, 9/11, 7/7, governmental legislation
such as the *Incitement to Religious Hatred Bill*. Third, factors such
as anniversaries, like Wilberforce and 1807, which we have
squeezed for all their worth, realizing perhaps for the first time
that social reform and evangelistic zeal can complement each
other, and scratching our heads as to why we have not seen this
before.

Current examples of evangelical public theology
What does this resurfacing look like? On a more localized
level some churches and church networks that in the past have
been suspicious of social involvement have started to engage in
social welfare and development projects, under what might

---

21. From within these disciplines, I understand the need to approach such
    a topic within the context of continuing debates over secularization and
    sacralization, and then within a worldwide context: of the role of religion
    in the world, Christianity in the world, evangelicalism in the world, reli-
    gion in British public life, and Christianity in public life. For a helpful
    summary regarding these ever-decreasing contextual circles, see Coffey
    2004.

be more properly called 'diaconal' or 'mercy ministries'. On the transdenominational and sociopolitical systemic level we have seen the continuing work and increased profile and influence of various groups.[22]

We have also seen a spate of new initiatives. *Theos: A Public Theology Think-Tank*[23] was launched in 2005 and received some media interest. It

> exists to undertake research and provide commentary on social and political arrangements. The word 'Theos' and our descriptor, 'the public theology think tank', reflect our overall aim of putting God 'back' into the public domain. Theos is about social, public theology; about public wisdom.
>
> (Spencer 2006: 2)

Their inaugural piece of research is their report *Doing God: A Future for Faith in the Public Square*, authored by Nick Spencer, who writes that the aim of the report is

> a rubble-clearing exercise, an attempt to clear away some objections to letting God into the public square and to create a space for public theology by arguing why religious engagements in public debates should, and in all probability will, increase in 21st century Britain.
>
> (2006: 67).

---

22. Such as the Jubilee Centre / Relationship Foundations <http://www.jubilee-centre.org/; http://www.relationshipsfoundation. org/>, Christian Institute <http://www.christian.org.uk/home.htm>, Lawyers Christian Fellowship <http://www.lawcf.org/>, Church Society <http://www.churchsociety.org/index.asp>, London Institute of Contemporary Christianity <http://www.licc.org.uk/>, Christian Action and Research Network <http://www.care.org.uk/>, Care for the family <http://www.careforthefamily.org.uk/>, Bible Society <http://www.biblesociety.org.uk/>, and, albeit from a different subculture, Faithworks <http://www.faithworks.info/> and Ekklesia <http://www.ekklesia.co.uk/>.

23. See http://www.theosthinktank.co.uk/.

Then there is the founding of the Kirby Laing Institute for
Christian Ethics based at Tyndale House, Cambridge, under the
direction of the political theorist Dr Jonathan Chaplin.[24] Last, but
by no means least, is the Evangelical Alliance's ambitious *Faith and
Nation: Report of a Commission of Inquiry* (Evangelical Alliance 2006),
three years in the making and 'a major contribution to the Alliance's
Movement for Change which seeks "to reinvigorate Christian
witness and make a significant impact on the moral and spiritual
heart of the nation"' (Evangelical Alliance 2006: 8). The Report
contains one hundred specific recommendations to the Evangelical
Alliance Council, generalized in the following challenge:

> What is needed for evangelicals to maximise their potential in the UK
> can be presented in the form of a fourfold challenge. Firstly, evangelical
> politics must be rooted in faith in the Lordship of Christ and the
> authority of the Bible. Secondly, evangelicals must face up to the need
> to produce greater expert analysis together with more sophisticated
> study and research. Thirdly, they need to work harder at co-operating
> with each other, as well as learning to work with others where
> appropriate. Fourthly, evangelicals need themselves to become far more
> engaged in aspects of public life on the ground.
>
> (136–137)[25]

Resurfacing and the danger of the bends

What are we to make of such initiatives and developments? The
emergence of more church-based welfare and development
projects is a positive sign, especially if behind the activity is a
questioning as to (1) whether the state has a 'God-given' (pun
intended) right to be automatic welfare providers and (2) the problems this can cause in perpetuating our dependency culture. What
must happen now, though, is more sophisticated thinking that
structurally evidences the relational dynamic between word and
deed, and evangelism and social action, which I outlined earlier.

---

24. See http://www.tyndale.cam.ac.uk/KLICE/.
25. Interestingly the Alliance has recently merged its theology and social
    affairs units into one department called 'Public Theology'.

First, as classical evangelicals we have some hard thinking to do on what Chester calls the 'contextualization of the gospel for the urban poor'.[26] Indeed one point Chester makes is whether just doing bolt-on 'projects' simply reinforces a culture and mentality of entitlement, dependency and victimhood, when we should rather be looking for participation in our community, where the 'evangelization of the heart' should be our central task (see also Chester and Timmis 2007: ch. 4). When this is done, both 'felt needs' and 'real needs' are seamlessly integrated:

> People come with presenting issues: anger, bitterness, parenting, shopping, addiction, economic need, depression, violence and so on. We need to do more than deal with these issues *as a context* for speaking the gospel. This treats things as separate issues: I help sort out someone's housing benefit in the hope that I might then have an opportunity to give them a gospel presentation or invite them to church. Instead we need to treat these presenting issues directly so they become ways into heart issues. We need to connect the gospel with the specifics of people's lives rather than, or as well as, starting with big metaphysical questions.
>
> (Chester, 'Evangelising the Heart', 6)

Second, is the question as to whether these diaconal ministries really come under the umbrella of 'public' theology,[27] for characteristically these church-based initiatives are still what the sociologist Robert Putnam calls 'church-centred *bonding*' (or exclusive) social capital, as opposed to 'community centred *bridging*' (or inclusive) social capital (Putnam 2000: 13, quoted in Coffey 2004: 100). This is of concern to some, such as the evangelical historian John Coffey who, regarding contemporary construals of the

---

26. Tim Chester, 'Evangelising the Heart: Contextualising the Gospel for the Urban Poor' (unpublished paper given to the author, Mar. 2007).

27. Remembering Chaplin's definition of 'public' quoted above: 'The public realm refers to that social space within which individuals and communities or associations interact with each other in ways that transcend their own unique rights and responsibilities.'

relationship between evangelicals and the state, places such activity under the category of the 'irrelevant State':

> Whereas mainline Protestants 'provided a disproportionate share of leadership to the wider civic community', Evangelicals tend to 'put more emphasis on church-centred activities'. We may wish to challenge Putnam's generalizations, but his argument should give us pause for thought. Clearly there is a danger in the liberal Protestant model, where Christian energies are invested in civic life at the expense of the church itself. But Evangelicals often tend toward the other extreme, shunning 'the world' and turning the church into a ghetto from which we rarely emerge. If being 'in the world, not of it' is the Christian's goal, then we need to ensure that believers are not only deeply rooted in the church but also actively involved in the life of the wider community. We need to rediscover an ethic of public service.
>
> (2004: 100)

At this point we come to a number of thorny ecclesiological questions. We desire to apply the whole counsel of God in this area, of which Galatians 6:10 is a microcosm, 'So then, as we have opportunity, let us do good to everyone, and especially to those who are of the household of faith.' But is it so easy to demarcate the church community and the community of which the church is a part? And even if fellow-believers are our primary responsibility,[28] how proactive or reactive are we to be concerning 'outsider' categories that the Bible speaks about: neighbours, strangers and enemies (see Keller 1989: 80–92).

Third, we need to reflect upon the type of social involvement our churches should be involved with. Among classical evangelicals, Keller has done more thinking than most in this area. In speaking about the church's vision in mercy ministry, he notes a number of factors as to why many evangelicals are happy to

---

28. 'A simple review of all biblical admonitions to help the poor reveals that most texts refer to poor brethren – to Christians . . . God puts the first responsibility for a poor man upon those in very closest covenant relationship with him' (Keller 1989: 81).

speak in terms of social welfare but nervous about social reform. For him, there is a middle-class captivity that blinds us to systemic and structural evil, and forgets that 'laws and policies must be changed *as well as* individuals . . . "Lordship evangelism" seeks to be "as pervasive as sin itself"; it addresses both selfish individuals *and* social systems with the gospel. Christians must not simply bandage the wound. They must also pursue the attacker' (1989: 176–177). Then there are the ideological biases to which evangelicals are captive, seen in either big government or big business: 'But both government and business should recognise that neither of them can take the place of the church, the family and voluntary associations in the fight against social problems' (178).

Keller proposes 'a model of seven concentric circles of intervention strategies' (181) under three wide-ranging headings: *Relief* (direct assistance, informational and counselling, advocacy), *Transformation* (individual, community) and *Reform* (information for justice; intervention for justice). Most relevant here are Keller's guiding principles concerning final circle, the intervention for justice, which fits most comfortably into our 'public theology' focus:

1. The church's work of transformation and even relief will certainly change social structures. It is not possible to draw a distinction between relief and reform. They lead to one another. If a ministry lifts up the poor in a community, it will drastically alter the order of things. Therefore it is mistaken to say that the church should not be seeking to change the shape of society.

2. The church cannot present unnecessary barriers to the inquirer after Christ . . . Churches that are too heavily invested in the political agenda of a particular party or candidate can appear to be captive to an ideology instead of the lordship of Christ . . . *For this reason, except in the most clear, broad, and basic public issues . . . , it is best for interventional social reform to be carried out by voluntary associations, parachurch groups, which can use political power to change social structure.*

(189; my emphasis)

I will return to the issue of 'who does what' at the conclusion of the chapter.

Concerning this sociopolitical level and our place in the public square, there are encouraging signs; for it has slowly dawned on us that there is no naked public square and, in fact, atheistic liberal humanism has set the rules of engagement, rules that must be unmasked and challenged as being as tradition-specific and exclusive as the traditions they seek to push to the margins. Indeed I believe we can afford to be even more belligerent in this deconstruction. 'Rubble-clearing' as Spencer calls it, needs heavy equipment and is by its nature a destructive work.

But now comes the problem; for after a demolition job, there is the need for a constructive building project. What do we propose to put in the place of what we have knocked down? At this point, and speaking as a theologian, as I survey many current attempts at evangelical public engagement, I become frustrated. I see that what is being proposed is rather flimsy and ramshackle, and certainly not following any clear theological blueprint. Although Spencer applies the following phrase more generally to the role of faith in the public square, I wonder whether the same can be said about evangelical public theology, 'a fudge wrapped in a muddle inside an uncertainty' (Spencer 2006: 17).

We are engaged, yes, but for widely different *reasons*, proposing widely different *solutions* and with widely different *aims, objectives and expectations*. Certainly theological terms and doctrines are used but often these verge on being sound bites taken out of their proper biblical-theological context. There seems to be very little unified comprehensive systemic meta-theological thinking that could act as a detailed blueprint for public theology.

As an aside here I note that while their foundations may be dangerously unstable, Roman Catholic public theology and social thinking look more impressive and substantial in comparison, a point the Evangelical Alliance's *Faith and Nation* report notes:

> Evangelicals are not renowned for authoritative, scholarly, sustained, theologically grounded thinking on complex social and political issues in ways that have characterised some other Christian traditions, such as, for

example, Roman Catholicism. Accordingly, it has not been unusual to find evangelical political engagement appearing somewhat fragmented, inconsistent, unbalanced and consequently ineffective.

(Evangelical Alliance 2006: 136)

At this point let us take one illustrative example of this evangelical diversity in public theology: our response to Islam in Britain. Compare and contrast these three statements, all from classical evangelicals but all of which display very different public theological presuppositions, not just about the religion of Islam, but also regarding culture and the nature of the state.

First, the conclusion of the report *Islam in Britain* written by the Institute for the Study of Islam and Christianity under the directorship of Dr Patrick Sookhdeo:

The Muslim community itself needs to address what it wants of Britain. Is it to replicate the Muslim-majority societies in the 'home countries' . . . or is it to enter fully into the life of mainstream Britain recognising that dramatic changes may be needed? Such changes would include the need for the individual to take precedence over the community, the privatisation of religion, and the abandoning of religious law. Muslims should seek to create a new, liberal form of British Islam, that rejects traditional notions of *jihad*, apostasy, subordination of non-Muslims and the seeking of Islamic supremacy, and reinterprets its sources in terms of human rights, tolerance, acceptance of minority status, secularist separation of religion from state, and adaptation to the values of the majority society . . . Muslim leaders must understand that, in order to enjoy the benefits of British citizenship, they should be willing to accept the level playing field of British democracy and British law, and integrate into society as a whole. They must give up any desire to create a separate, alternate autonomous community, living under special political, legal and economic arrangements within larger society. They must also give up any intention of transforming the UK into an Islamic state.

(Sookhdeo 2005: 135–136)

Second, Peter Leithart, in an article entitled 'Mirror of Christendom':

Islam's all-embracing vision is a rebuke to modern Christianity. Once
upon a time, Christians saw their faith as equally all-embracing . . .
That vision all but evaporated in modern Christianity . . . Whatever
plausibility structure Christendom provided has crumbled, and
millions of people now grow up in the former nations of
Christendom without the slightest exposure to Christianity in any
form. Christendom shed its Hebraic attachment to culture . . . At the
heart of the gospel is the announcement that Jesus, the Crucified One,
has been raised to be Lord of all. If that has happened, then, as Oliver
O'Donovan has argued at length, we should expect the nations to
become worshipers of this Lord. But Christians have largely given up
this expectation, and have certainly given up the demand that the
nations bow before the Son. We act as if the cross and resurrection
left the world unchanged. Point four on the to-do list: Revive
Christendom.

(Leithart 2007: 11–12)

Finally, David Holloway of the Christian Institute:

There is indeed a clash of civilizations in the world and in Britain. What
is currently being played out in Britain, however, is not a clash between
Islam and the West. Rather it is a clash between Islam, Christianity and a
secular decadent West, in which Christianity is in the middle. What is the
way ahead? It is vital that we preserve those freedoms that were secured
at the end of the 17th century after the Wars of Religion. In simple
terms it was then agreed that no longer could the State enforce any
religious belief. Nevertheless the State still could and must outlaw
violence and sexual immorality. That meant in Britain that under an
overarching Christian establishment there could be subordinate
pluralisms. Of course, secularists are happy with outlawing violence and
Muslims happy with outlawing sexual immorality. But Muslims must
renounce violence more than they seem to be doing at present and
secularists must work for a change in sexual behaviour and the
reinstitutionalization of marriage. And with freedom secured, there can
be open debate over the truth claims of each world view or 'civilization'.
Then, as Christians, we must speak the truth in love, as it is, and only is,
in Jesus.

(Holloway 2007: no p.)

My definition of 'evangelical public theology' includes both reflection and engagement. With the resurfacing of the evangelical mind in matters of public life comes the danger of what one might call the 'theological bends'. We wish to react and engage, and we must, but if we do this too quickly without the necessary theological reflection, by which of course I mean 'right' reflection, the results will continue to be confused and counterproductive. (I am told that the way to avoid the bends is proper training, good equipment and careful execution.)

Such deficient or absent reflection may in part be understandable. The majority of those engaged in the public square are activists and practitioners, with a God-given sense of vocation to use the gifts they have been given to glorify God. They are probably frustrated with people like me who are always reflecting but never engaging: always *in* the college, but never *out* there in the world. They are probably frustrated with many evangelical pastor/teachers, in that they have not felt particularly encouraged in their vocation, let alone been given the theological world view to think 'Christianly' about their vocation. My plea here is that as brothers and sisters working together in the Body of Christ, we help each other more.

The last part of this chapter is an attempt to help, showing some theological workings: what I believe to be the major theological decisions we need to take in providing *an* overarching framework for evangelical public theology before sketching in barest form what I believe to be *the* two most viable frameworks. Both of these frameworks are tradition-specific, using the grammar and vocabulary of the Reformed Evangelical faith.

Building a theological framework

Doctrinal foundations
Let us start with the raw systematic and biblical-theological material we must fashion. I am presuming here that the following components will be most relevant in our construction, are exegetically founded in Scripture and are familiar to us. First, we have God's general revelation in nature and God's 'worded' special revelation,

both of which in their own distinctive ways and for their own
distinctive purposes are necessary, authoritative, sufficient and per-
spicuous (see Van Til 1946). A corollary here is God's moral
standard/norm, his law both revealed in general revelation and
special revelation. Second, is the overarching world historical
pattern of creation, fall, redemption, consummation and some
important 'glueing' doctrines that join them together, the concept
of 'covenant' with its blessings and curses, and 'kingdom' with its
rulers and realms.

Under 'creation' I mention again the cultural mandate, and also
structural or institutional pluralism: that is to say, God has ordered
the world so that under his supreme authority there are other
authorities (church, family and state), each with its own unique
responsibilities and sanctions.

Under 'fall' we must reckon anthropologically with the complementary truths of the 'antithesis', common grace and the image of
God. The 'antithesis' is God's judicial curse sovereignly inflicted
on humanity in Genesis 3:15, which, from then until now, puts
enmity between followers of God and followers of Satan at all
levels, intellectual and moral, individual and societal. The antithesis
is *principally* 'the diametrical opposition between belief and unbelief and therefore between belief and any compromise of revealed
truth' (Frame 1995: 188). The Bible presents this stark contrast
between belief and unbelief in many ways: light and dark, death
and life, those who are blind and those who can see, covenant
keepers and covenant breakers, those in Adam and those in Christ.
As Jesus says, 'Whoever is not with me is against me' (Matt. 12:30)
and 'No one can serve two masters' (Matt. 6:24).

I stress *principally* because, as well as affirming the truth of the
antithesis, we must affirm two other biblical truths. First, as believers, we know in practice that a version of the antithesis still runs
through our own hearts as we daily deal with our indwelling sin,
sin that is a contradiction according to who we are in Christ.
Second, we note a similar inconsistency in the unbeliever. As the
theologian Cornelius Van Til put it:

> The natural man, 'sins against' his own essentially Satanic principle. As
> the Christian has the incubus of his 'old man' weighing him down and

therefore keeping him from realizing the 'life of Christ' within him, so
the natural man has the incubus of the sense of Deity weighing him
down and keeping him from realizing the life of Satan within him. The
actual situation is therefore always a mix of truth with error. Being
'without God in the world' the natural man yet knows God, and, in spite
of himself, to some extent recognizes God. By virtue of their creation in
God's image, by virtue of the ineradicable sense of deity within them
and by virtue of God's restraining general grace, those who hate God,
yet in a restricted sense know God, and do good.

(Van Til 1974: 27)

As well as the 'antithesis' we must affirm God's non-salvific
common grace, his goodness showered on a sin-cursed world. In
common grace God restrains his own wrath and restrains sin
and its consequences in unbelievers, and also positively blesses
creation and excites the unbeliever to perform works of civic
righteousness. We must also affirm that all men and women are
made in the image of God, that their very being reveals the God
who is, and that no matter how much they claim otherwise and try
to deface this image, they can never totally succeed. The idols they
necessarily fashion in creation and in the mind are distorted and
perverted copies and counterfeits of the living God whom they
know but do not know.

One scholar who is able to capture this anthropological com-
plexity is the Dutch missiologist J. H. Bavinck. In his *Church
Between Temple and Mosque* Bavinck gives a wonderful exposition of
Romans 1:18–32, touching on these issues. He says:

Man has repressed the truth of the everlasting power of the divinity of
God. It has been exiled to the unconscious, to the crypts of his existence.
That does not mean, however, that it has vanished forever. Still active, it
reveals itself again and again. But it cannot become openly conscious; it
appears in disguise, and it is exchanged for something different. Thus, all
kinds of ideas of God are formed; the human mind as the *fabrica idolorum*
(Calvin) makes its own ideas of God and its own myths. This is not
intentional deceit – it happens without man knowing it. He cannot get rid
of these ideas and myths. So he has religion; he is busy with a god; he
serves his god – but he does not see that the god he serves is not God

himself. An exchange has taken place, a perilous exchange. An essential
quality of God has been blurred because it did not fit in with the human
pattern of life, and the image man has of God is no longer true. Divine
revelation indeed lies at the root of this image, but man's thoughts and
aspirations cannot receive it and adapt themselves to it. In the image man
has of God we can recognize the image of man himself.

(Bavinck 1966: 122)

Under 'redemption' we have the significance of Christ's life,
death, resurrection, ascension and continuing session for *all* of
creation, the Great Commission to disciple all nations and some
version of an 'inaugurated eschatology' (the now and not-yet),
although, of course, shaped by one's millennial sensibilities. Finally,
under 'consummation' we affirm the physicality of the new heaven
and the new earth.[29]

Doctrinal differences

So far, I hope, we have a general agreement concerning these
contours. Now come the differences as we configure, stress,
emphasize, accent and nuance the above in different ways and start
to join the dots. One helpful way to understand these differences is
viewing them as a set of interconnected relationships of continuity and discontinuity.[30] What is the continuity and/or discontinuity
between creation and redemption, between the cultural mandate
and the gospel mandate, between the creation and new creation
this side of Judgment Day and the new heaven and new earth the
other side? Typologically and hermeneutically what is the continuity and discontinuity between Old Covenant and New Covenant,
Old Testament Israel and the church of Christ, Old Testament
Israel and the nations, between the Mosaic law, the royal law, and
law written on the heart?

As one plots where one stands on all these questions, I suggest
that there will begin to appear in outline form two related but quite

---

29. For a general introduction here, see Hoekema 1979

30. Remembering that in a larger theological context and compared to, say,
    dispensationalism, Reformed theology is itself a model of continuity.

distinct 'visions' for public theology; indeed there is a sibling rivalry between the two. Both claim to have a rich historical pedigree (indeed both claim to be heirs of Calvin), and both have their sophisticated contemporary interpreters, all of which give their own variations on a theme. I can do little more than bash out the basic melody of both and then offer some brief reasons why I think one may be more in tune with Scripture than the other.

Presenting two models for consideration

A 'two kingdoms' model: discontinuity
The first is a 'two kingdoms' model and is, I contend, a self-conscious articulation of what much classical evangelical public theology unconsciously falls into. The phrase 'two kingdoms' is usually associated with Lutheranism, what Richard Niebuhr well describes as 'Christ and culture in paradox' (Niebuhr 2001). As the Augsburg Confession of Faith states:

> Christ's kingdom is spiritual; it is knowledge of God in the heart, the fear of God and faith, the beginning of eternal righteousness and eternal life. At the same time it lets us make outward use of the legitimate political ordinances of the nation in which we live, just as it lets us make use of medicine or architecture, food or drink or air. The gospel does not introduce any new laws about the civil estate, but commands us to obey existing laws, whether they were formulated by heathens or by others, and in obedience to practice love.
>
> (Augsburg Confession [1530], Article 16: 'Of Political Order')

While there are some resemblances to the Lutheran formulation, a Reformed 'two kingdoms' model uses Reformed doctrines in its articulation. On the 'Reformed' version of the continuity/discontinuity question, the 'two-kingdoms' model can be called a model of discontinuity and dichotomy. It can be described as follows.

God is sovereign, Jesus is Lord and King over all, the Bible is our ultimate authority and yet God exercises his rule in two different ways, in two different realms, with two different norms and with two different expectations for each realm. God is Creator and Sustainer (but not Redeemer) of the 'civil realm', a realm that pertains to temporal, earthly, provisional matters, not matters of ultimate and spiritual importance. The other realm is the 'spiritual realm', where God is Creator, sustainer and redeemer in Christ, 'this kingdom pertains to things that are of ultimate spiritual importance, the things of Christ's heavenly, eschatological kingdom' (Van Drunen 2006: 24). Concerning the relationship of the two, says Van Drunen, 'although necessarily existing together and having some mutual interaction in this world, these two kingdoms enjoy a great measure of independence so that each can pursue the unique work entrusted to it' (24).

From the perspective of biblical theology we can say that from the fall, and running in parallel with redemptive history, is a God-ordained common cultural history, made up of both covenant-keepers and covenant-breakers and sustained by God's common grace. Redemptive history, and all it contains in terms of Israel, law, society covenantal sanctions of blessings and cursings, is an anomaly, a typological 'intrusion' of the eschatological kingdom to come, where there will be total separation of covenant-keepers and covenant-breakers, a true theocracy. As Meredith Kline notes:

> Apropos of the fifth word [commandment], it is in this New Testament
> age not a legitimate function of a civil government to endorse and
> support religious establishments. This principle applies equally to the
> Christian church; for though its invisible government is theocratic with
> Christ sitting on David's throne in the heavens and ruling over it, yet its
> visible organization, in particular as it is related to civil powers, is so
> designed that it takes a place of only common privilege along with other
> religious institutions within the framework of common grace.
>
> (Kline 1972: 167)

In a 'two kingdoms' approach evangelical public theology concerns this mixed common-cultural history; the 'civil realm' and the godly realm have their own norm and moral basis. A 'two kingdoms' approach appreciates and appropriates a version of 'natural law' given in general revelation, the law written on the heart, common to all humanity and the moral basis for civic morality and the common good.[31] It is argued that Scripture at this point is an 'insufficient' basis in the civil realm, but that Scripture mandates its own insufficiency. Natural law will also prove to be tactically and strategically more persuasive to unbelievers. Ken Myers notes:

> Telling a late-20th century pagan that he has disobeyed God's word is likely to have little rhetorical power. Telling him that he has, in C. S. Lewis' terms, gone 'against the grain of the universe' might well pack a bit more rhetorical punch, especially if the inevitability of cosmic splinters is spelled out. In a culture that tends to regard all rules and all religion as merely conventional, biblical law language is horribly easy to ignore.
>
> (Myers 1994: 61)

A two-kingdoms approach sees a looser connection than some between culture and cult, between the shape of a society and the religious presuppositions underlying that society. There is no distinctively Christian culture or Christian civilization, and while the 'secularist' state is an enemy of the civil realm, the 'secular' state is a definition of the 'civil realm', one of the triumphs of the West. Daryl Hart is a strong advocate of this position:

> The Christian religion was planted and grew in cultural soils that were already well tilled and flourishing. It did not need to hatch a new culture or civilization from scratch. Even when it did, its contributions to the West fed off existing arrangements, at least from the Romans if not the Greeks. Second, even more important is that lack of teaching either by Christ or the apostles that the new religion was to be the basis for Christian culture or society. Here the relationship of Christianity to Judaism might explain why Christ would say his kingdom was not of this world. For Christians, the patterns of theocracy were no longer valid after the coming of Christ. Christians need not try to replicate Israel's legitimate attempt to integrate cult and culture but were permitted to live hyphenated-lives, as Greek-Christians, Jewish-Christians,

---

31. For some contemporary defences of a Reformed version of natural law, see Budziszewski 1997, Van Drunen 2006 and Grabhill 2006.

Roman-Christians, and more. In other words, Christian teachings gave
no instruction on the establishment of a distinctly Christian culture
because Christianity was a religion without a specific land, city, or place.
Its teaching transcended that cult–culture relationship as faith for people
from any ethnic background.

(Hart 2006: 250–251)

Finally, while we are not to be indifferent, culturally, economically
or socially, the two-kingdoms model

demands limited and sober expectations. This perspective gives no
reason to expect the attainment of paradise on earth . . . The civil
kingdom, regulated by natural law, is severely limited in what it can attain,
but Scripture gives us no reason to expect more from it.

(Van Drunen 2006: 40–41)

It has a relative importance in the maintenance of order and
restraining of evil. So as Christians, we live 'hyphenated lives' as
citizens of both kingdoms, but as aliens, pilgrims and exiles, our
true longing is for our spiritual home:

The otherworldly character of Christianity . . . should lower the stakes
of politics for those in the church. Of course such otherworldliness may
also produce political indifference. But with a properly high estimate of
the created order, human nature, and the relative importance of civil
society for maintaining order and restraining evil (at least), Christians
may fruitfully participate in public life not as a site of redemption but as
an essential part of their humanity. Secular politics need not compromise
Christian identity . . . secular politics is thoroughly compatible with
orthodox Christianity.

(Hart 2006: 257)

The two-kingdoms model would appear to exclude both theologically and psychologically any version of the postmillennial
hope. As someone provocatively remarked to me recently, while
we are to enjoy God's creation and engage in culture, from the perspective of eternity our cultural endeavours are akin to 'a lick of
paint in a cancer ward'.

Indeed, going further, Hart warns against Reformed Christians speaking in terms of our desire to 'transform' society, because with it comes the twin temptations of triumphalism and social Christianity ('Where life in this world begins to look more important than preparation for the life to come' [Hart 1999: 7]), temptations he believes the Reformed community is prone to yield to. Rather Calvinists should be more Lutheran:

> Obviously, the humility taught by the theology of the cross and the doctrine of the two kingdoms puts a strong break [sic] upon conceiving Christianity as the transformation of culture. Lutheranism especially teaches that God is gaining victory not through human accomplishments in making a better world, but through the suffering and toil of our pilgrimage here. Could it be in fact, that the aggressiveness associated with a Reformed world-and-life view is a form of the theology of glory to which the Corinthian church aspired? The Corinthians wanted a return to the glory days of Israel and could not see that God had accomplished far more through the cross of Christ . . .
>
> (1999: 7)

A 'transformationist' model: continuity

The second model is what I will call the 'transformationist' model. Here God is sovereign, Jesus is Lord and King over all, the Bible is our ultimate authority and God commands that this be acknowledged by everyone, in every sphere of life. On the 'Reformed' version of the continuity/discontinuity question, this model can be called a model of continuity and unity. While still upholding structural/institutional pluralism (i.e. not confusing or conflating, church, state, family), transformationist models join aspects they believe the 'two kingdoms' falsely dichotomize: earthly and heavenly, physical and spiritual, judicial-covenantal and material, individual and cosmic, civil and religious, God's law in one realm of life and his law in another.

From the broadest perspective redemption should be seen as restoration of creation in all its many spheres: 'redemption is not an ontological transformation, but an ethical reorientation and redirection' (M. Williams 1992: 15). Because Christ's work is *the* significant event in history, what one writer calls 'the transition from wrath to grace' (North 1990: 3), less stress is to be put on the discontinuity between the earth now and the new heaven and new earth, because the new creation, inaugurated by Christ's resurrection, has begun in history. Therefore, rather than thinking of ourselves as 'resident aliens', might it be more accurate to think of ourselves as 'alienated residents' (Hegeman 1999: 88)? And when one's framework encompasses the movement from Paradise lost to Paradise regained, and when one recognizes the physicality and continuity between now and not-yet, this will motivate us to start working as soon as we are converted. Anthony Hoekema puts it like this:

> As citizen's of God's kingdom, we may not just write off the present
> earth as a total loss, or rejoice in its deterioration. We must indeed be
> working for a better world now. Our efforts to bring the kingdom of
> Christ into fuller manifestation are of eternal significance. Our Christian
> life today, our struggles against sin – both individual and institutional –
> our mission work, our attempt to develop and promote a distinctively
> Christian culture, have value not only for this world but even for the
> world to come . . . Only eternity will reveal the full significance of what
> has been done for Christ here.
>
> (Hoekema 1979: 287)

Plantinga catches this vision nicely in his description of the relationship between church and commonwealth:

> The Calvinist and Reformed concept of the commonwealth is linked to
> the doctrine of the kingdom of God by being the kingdom's slowly
> realised, still imperfect, but proleptic expression. In the end at the last
> judgment, Jesus Christ the Lord completely 'restores' and 'renews' the
> whole world. He restores a completely 'just order'. The kingdom of God
> or Christ is cosmic in scope and utterly invincible. All things *will* be made
> new. With a Marxist-like paradox of zeal for the inevitable, the church
> serves as a witness to the new order, as agent for it, and as first model or
> exemplar of it. For the decisive turn has already been taken in the work of
> Christ. This is preached and witnessed to by the proclamation of the word:
> . . . sin has been abolished, salvation has been given back to men, and in
> short the whole world has been renewed and all things restored to order.
>
> (Plantinga 1983: 203)

Another way of looking at this is the 'conceptual congruence' between cultural mandate and Great Commission.

> The Great Commission is the republication of the cultural mandate for the semi-eschatological age. Unlike the original cultural mandate, it presupposes the existence of sin and the accomplishment of redemption. It recognises that if the world is to be filled with worshipers of God, subduing the earth as his vassal kings, they must first be converted to Christ through the preaching of the gospel.
>
> (Frame 2007: 288)

Transformation should not and will not come about by imposed morality, but by men and women being converted and willingly submitting themselves to the King of kings and his rule.

Concerning revelation, transformationist models are far less happy to separate general revelation and special revelation, natural law and biblical law. Both are needed, and have always been needed, to interpret the other. Transformationists recognize the personal knowledge of God all unbelievers have by virtue of their being made in God's image, and yet tend to stress more the antithesis between believer and unbeliever, and the inextricable link between cult (the worship of the living God or the worship of idols) and culture (which is the externalization of that worship). That is to say, the noetic effects of the fall are so damaging and debilitating that general revelation, without the clarity and regenerating power of special revelation, is severely limited and is unstable ground for moral consensus. Leithart is one writer critical of a Reformed version of natural law:

> On these epistemological questions, advocates of natural law have displayed an odd ambivalence. Recent advocates claim that it is useless to appeal to God's law when speaking to a modern pagan. Ken Myers has recently written that 'telling a late-20th-century pagan that he has disobeyed God's word is likely to have little rhetorical power.' If all men know God naturally, however, an appeal to God's law would seem to be entirely appropriate. Natural law theory resists the proposition that all men *know* the one true God. Instead, it tends to assert that all men have a sense that some 'supreme being' exists, and know something *about* the

character of this supreme being. This is far less than Paul claims. Paul
claims that all men *know* (in the personal sense; not merely know about)
God (the One True God, Father, Son and Holy Spirit). They may not
know Him by name, but it is He whom they know. In this respect, the
problem with natural law is not that it claims too *much* for natural
knowledge, but that it claims too *little*. Speaking Christianly to an
unbeliever is not like speaking Swahili to a Swede; it is like speaking
Swedish to an American of Swedish descent who has almost, but not
quite, forgotten his native tongue.

On the other hand, natural law claims too much for the ability of
those who are outside Christ to embrace and put into practice what they
know. The fact that men know the moral law does not, for Paul, lead to
the conclusion that natural morality is sufficient as far as it goes. On the
contrary, because the natural man suppresses and distorts the knowledge
he cannot escape, natural morality is ultimately foolish and darkness.

(Leithart 1996: 19–20)

The Bible is both sufficient and necessary to equip the Christian
for *every* good work, which includes the cultural and political
spheres. Common grace is affirmed, but as a *description* of God's
goodness in causing the sinner to be inconsistent in his thinking
and acting, rather than being a *prescription* of what culture should
look like in its movement from Garden to Garden City. Indeed
what is often taken as evidence of general revelation, natural law
and common grace in our Western culture may actually be rather
the historical influence of special revelation, biblical law and the
gospel. This is Leithart's thesis in his paper *Did Plato Read Moses?*:

I hope to make a plausible case that much of what has been identified as
a moral consensus based on natural revelation is more accurately seen as
a product of general and special revelation. Pagans hold to certain moral
principles that are compatible with Christian morality not only because
they are inescapably confronted with God's revelation in creation, but also
because they have been directly or indirectly exposed to and influenced by
the Spirit operating though special revelation and the other means of
grace. Whatever moral consensus exists is thus not a product of pure
'common grace' (devoid of all contact with revelation), nor of 'special
grace' (saving knowledge of God through Christ and his word), but what

I call . . . 'middle grace' (non-saving knowledge of God and his will
derived from both general and special revelation. To put it another way,
because of the cultural influence of the Bible, unbelievers in America are
more Christian than unbelievers in Irian Jaya. To put it another way, there
is and has never existed a pure 'common grace' cultural situation.

(Leithart 1995: 4–5)

Like a two-kingdoms approach, the 'secularist' state will be an enemy
to be opposed; unlike the two-kingdoms approach, the 'secular'
state is seen to be a 'myth', a confused, compromised and unstable
state of affairs, and a fruit of the Enlightenment rather than the
Reformation.[32] For transformationists, the concept of Christendom
is by no means anathema (see e.g. Leithart 2003: ch. 5).

Finally, and before I conclude, what are the expectations of
transformationists? Here, as elsewhere, one's eschatological commitments play a large part in answering this question. I believe one
can construct versions of transformation that cover a range of
Reformed eschatological views. Whatever our short-, or long-term
expectations, whatever transformation we see, or do not see, we
are called to be faithful and to be faithful in our callings.

On being 'offensive' and 'thick' in public

Given these two models, 'two kingdoms' and 'transformationist',
I tend toward a version of the transformation model for a variety
of reasons. One reason is that this model is able to justify the proclamation of the evangel in every part of life without apology or
embarrassment. The issue is not about whether or not for the sake
of strategy and/or communication we use non-biblical language in
the public square, for we can and should, and it certainly does not
mean we have to quote the Bible after every cultural or political
utterance. Rather it is a theological presupposition underlying our
engagement that pushes me toward transformation. Leithart puts
it well:

---

32. See the chapter by David Field in this volume.

If one believes that the gospel does not directly address political and cultural concerns, then one can appeal to standards of political behaviour without reference to the gospel. Witness can be sharply separated from political-cultural speech; we can safely become bilingual. If the gospel embraces politics, if the gospel includes the political claim that Jesus Christ is enthroned as King of Kings and Lord of Lords, then it should be evident that the Christian has nothing to say to political actors that can stand on its own, apart from the gospel. To accept the first alternative is to bind the gospel in the straightjacket of the modern public/private distinction. It is to deny that the gospel is, as Leslie Newbigin put it, 'public truth'.

(Leithart 1996: 28)

For those evangelicals nervous that engaging in evangelical public theological tasks might detract from evangelism, I suggest that a transformational model will provide *more* opportunities to speak about the gospel, for we will realize that there is no area in life which is epistemologically and ethically neutral, that following the Maker's instructions actually works and that as Christians we can explain *why*. Finally, speaking the truth in love, we can go on the offensive and argue that for autonomous rebellious unbelievers any order, structure and goodness in their life cannot be ultimately explained by them, and that they can only make sense of this by coming on to our territory, borrowing Christian capital. Of course, what I have just described here is nothing more than a presuppositional apologetic method applied more broadly to societal engagement. With discernment and wisdom we will be looking for opportunities to speak in the 'thick' language of Christian particularity rather than a 'thin' discourse, because we will want to give a reason for the hope we have in the gospel.

Conclusion: moving forward by stepping back

My aim in this chapter has not been to try to convince you of a transformationist model over a two-kingdoms model in doing evangelical public theology; indeed I would be worried if one were so easily persuaded either way on such a simplistic presentation of the positions. Rather my more modest aim has been to show the theological work and workings that lie behind evangelical public theology, remembering that we have always been engaged in public theology questions, because such questions are simply unavoidable. I hope this chapter may enable us to move forward by taking a step back to reflect more systemically upon these larger meta-theological questions, questions that ask, 'What on earth?', 'Why on earth?' and 'How on earth?'

Finally, and on the level of praxis, I ask one more question: '*Who* on earth?' Practically what does all this mean for each of us as disciples of the Lord Jesus Christ? What am I saying for you to do? In our social engagement and public theology, who does what? What do we do? More pointedly must I change what I am already doing?

To the last question, my answer is a firm no–yes. At this point it will be both extremely helpful and avoid unnecessary confusion (and inactivity) to remember the crucial distinction between 'church' and 'Church', between what Kuyper calls the church as 'institute' and the church as 'organism',[33] between 'church as a church in the world', and 'Christians in the world'.[34] Regarding the church as 'institute', the 'Church', we can say that there is a prescribed and limited sphere of operation:

> The task of the Church is to preach the gospel, to administer the sacraments, to apply Christian discipline, and to extend Christian mercy. The Word is preached to those who know and believe it in order to build them up as disciples of Christ and citizens of his kingdom and to give comfort. The Word is also preached to those who do not yet know Christ so that they may believe and become members of the body of Christ. The Church as a whole as well as every member has a part in this.
>
> (Tuit 2006: 133)

However, the 'church' (i.e. Christians) must also be seen as 'organism'. As Bolt notes:

---

33. On Kuyper's teaching here, see J. Bolt 2001: 427–428.
34. Carson 2008 has a helpful section on this distinction.

In Kuyper's view, Christians who go out into their various vocations do
so neither as direct emissaries of the institutional church nor as mere
individual believers . . . Christian social, cultural, and political action does
not flow directly from the structures and authorities of the church, but
come to expression organically in the various spheres of life as believers
live out the faith and spirituality that develops and is nurtured in the
church's worship and discipline.

(J. Bolt 2001: 429)

Comparing these two perspectives, Tuit again is helpful:

The church as institution does not have to be all things to all men, yet
the believer living in the different spheres does. The believer serves
Christ in the world in every area of life. The ministry of the church to
believers does impact every area of life but does not encompass it.

(Tuit 2000: 187)

The Kuyperian statement that every square inch of life belongs to Christ
cannot be applied to the institutional Church. Consequently, the
leadership of the pastor is a special kind of leadership in close
connection with the idea of office and the Word. The believer is
accountable to God for the Christian leadership he gives in society as a
citizen of the Kingdom guided by the Word preached and taught by the
'church' leader, the pastor. One could say therefore that the life of the
believer is mission, within the context of the cultural and the mission
mandate, rather than that the church is mission.

(Tuit 2006: 137 n. 56)[35]

For those called by God to serve and glorify him in the vocations to which you have been called, I ask that you do just that.
This means, surrounded by prayer, and steeling yourselves for the

---

35. Compare this to Peter Bolt's comments regarding the 'mission of the
church': 'The concept of the "mission" of the church ought to be laid to
rest. Acts does not present "the church" as an institution which is sent. A
particular church may send individuals to do a particular work (cf. 13:1–4),
but the church itself is not sent' (P. Bolt 1998: 211).

consequences of 'world view clash', you will take the time to think Christianly, not idolatrously, about how you are doing what you are doing and why you are doing it. You will be faithfully seeking to make sure that both the cultural mandate and Great Commission are being furthered in your particular vocation when you 'take every thought captive to obey Christ' (2 Cor. 10:5).

What about those called to be leaders in the local church? Although complex, we must discern what public theology tasks are appropriate for our churches *as churches* to be involved in, and get involved. As church leaders, we will be doing all we can to encourage, support and equip those under our care in the vocations to which they have been called in God's world. We will readily want to apply our preaching and teaching to matters of public life. Finally, we will look out for and relish opportunities to speak on public issues in our community, not simply because they are evangelistic opportunities but because we actually have something constructive to say on these issues: they are gospel issues because the gospel is public truth.

© Daniel Strange, 2008

2. NEW LIVING IN AN OLD CREATION

Kirsten Birkett

Introduction

Is full-time gospel preaching the only thing worth doing? Should Christians be involved in social justice and public service? Or is that genuinely a waste of time because all such structures 'will burn in the end'? Is a Christian carrying out his secular work with diligence and honesty doing something that is 'just as good' as full-time gospel preaching? Or do we have two classes of Christian: those in gospel work, and those doing anything else?

For some time now, evangelicals have pondered these questions. Some talk of the debate as 'kingdom ethics' versus 'creation ethics'. That is, we have a creation mandate from Genesis 1: to fill and subdue the earth, ruling in God's image, a mandate to work the garden that carries on after the fall, albeit in a more hostile environment. But then we also now have a kingdom mandate, since Jesus has come; that is, to preach the gospel, to grow the kingdom. Does this supersede the previous one? How should we regard the two?

Oliver O'Donovan is one English theologian with some important things to say in this debate, in a book not about evangelism but about the basis for evangelical ethics: *Resurrection and Moral Order* (O'Donovan 1994).[1] A very important thread of the book is on the topic 'creation or kingdom?' O'Donovan's answer is neither; not creation ethics, not kingdom ethics; it is resurrection ethics.

O'Donovan writes in his preface that he found courses in Christian ethics lacking in moral *theology* as their basis. He wrote his book, therefore, to provide an outline of theological ethics: systematic, not apologetic. While it was written neither to be a historical work nor contemporary debate, the preface to the second edition does contain a brief discussion as to how O'Donovan's work is positioned in relation to some current alternatives, and in the process outlines three principles on which his moral theology depends.

First is the *realist principle*: purposeful action is determined by what is true about the world into which we act. This is opposed to radical voluntarism, and distinguishes O'Donovan's work from, for instance, the ethical theory of John Finnis.[2] Second is the *evangelical principle*: truth is constituted by what God has done for his world and for humankind in Jesus Christ.[3] Third is the *Easter principle*: the act of God that liberates our action is focused on the resurrection of Jesus from the dead, which restored and fulfilled the intelligible order of creation.

It is in the Easter principle that we find O'Donovan's contribution to our current topic of interest. O'Donovan is concerned to

---

1. The following is in no sense a summary of this book, but rather a description of that part of O'Donovan's argument that addresses the particular tension between creation and kingdom ethics.

2. For Finnis's views, see Finnis 1983 and 1991, both of which are worth reading for those interested in gaining an understanding of current ethical debates.

3. O'Donovan contrasts this to the work of German theologian Martin Honecker, who accepts the realist principle, but says not all reality is evangelical reality. In particular, the reality from which we derive ethics is not. Rather it is the backdrop against which redemption appears in dialectical contrast. See O'Donovan 1994: xii.

overcome the conflict between creation ethics and kingdom ethics.
Both partial truths are included in the resurrection, where creation
is restored and fulfilment promised. However, after publication of
the first edition, some critics, such as Stanley Hauerwas, read this
as using the resurrection as a way back to creation ethics.

Now O'Donovan agrees with Hauerwas that creation order is
not self-evident. Their difference is in how to discover the truth
about it. Where Hauerwas, an Anglo-Catholic, turns to the *church*,
the Protestant O'Donovan turns to the *Christ-event*. Also, Hauerwas
has more emphasis on the crucifixion than other parts of the
'Christ-event'. O'Donovan is wary of misconceptions of the true
world order that Christians may take up – and one could be the
order in which martyrdom and asceticism are valued in themselves.

Besides, it is not *just* a matter of creation, reconciliation and
redemption, neat though that is. The Gospels also tell of advent.
Christian thought must take in all the moments of the Christ-
event. But even granting that, what is the significance of the
resurrection? Christian faith corresponds to the advent moment;
Christian obedient suffering, prayer and prophecy are part of conformity to Christ; but Christian *action* depends on the resurrection
moment, 'which vindicates the creation into which our actions can
be ventured with intelligibility' (O'Donovan 1994: xviii).

Therefore, we might say, ethics is about what we do when we
act freely and truthfully. That depends on resurrection above all
other theological points.

The importance of resurrection ethics

Christian ethics, O'Donovan insists, must arise from the gospel of
Jesus Christ. Otherwise, it could not be Christian ethics. Separating
faith in Christ from ethics leads to moralism or antinomianism.

> A belief in Christian ethics is a belief that certain ethical and moral
> judgements belong to the gospel itself; a belief, in other words, that the
> church can be committed to ethics without moderating the tone of its
> voice as a bearer of glad tidings.

(12)

Christian ethics is not midway between legalism and libertarianism. It is the opposite of both, since both are ways of living according to the flesh, taking responsibility for oneself, rather than in the Spirit.

So far so good. However, it is still too imprecise to say ethics arises from the gospel. How? What is the logic? The logic is, O'Donovan proposes, that *Christian ethics depends upon the resurrection of Jesus from the dead.*

The resurrection is, first of all (in O'Donovan's terms), God's reversal of Adam's choice of sin and death (1 Cor. 15:22), and, in the second place, a new affirmation of God's first decision for Adam to live. It is proof, then, that creation is not a lost cause. For O'Donovan, making resurrection the starting point is not to separate it from Jesus' death and ascension – both are crucial. But the centre is the confirmation of God's world order. Man's life on earth is important to God. We do put off the old because we have died; we also look forward to the end beyond. But without the resurrection this just becomes gnostic other-worldliness.

Which leads us to the dilemma of creation ethics as opposed to kingdom ethics. This, says O'Donovan, is not a right dichotomy. The very act that ushers in the kingdom also reaffirms creation. True kingdom ethics and true creation ethics have to be the same thing. Ethics that starts from the resurrection sometimes emphasizes the newness and sometimes the primitiveness of the order; but neither is denied.[4]

Christian ethics, O'Donovan goes on to say, is not esoteric nor optional. Since the Enlightenment, Western ethics has been largely voluntarist: morality is a creation of man's will. Moral reasoning has, therefore, been subservient to will: moral clashes come down to irreconcilable commitments. This suits irrationalist Christianity (writers such as Søren Kierkegaard). It also means Christian morality has no bearing on non-Christians; but it fails to reckon with

---

4. And, we might add, neither is completely relevant now; ethics will change in the new creation (there will be no marriage); ethics have changed from the original creation (singleness is now good). And all of the time we have new-creation ethics in an old-creation body; hence our struggle.

creation. Christian ethics actually is objective; there *is* human
nature, there *is* created order, even if both are distorted. Man per-
sistently rejects the created order, and is also inescapably confused
in his perception of it, so we cannot have a Stoic 'life in accord
with nature': anything we know about the good in created order
is revealed, not perceived. 'It is not, as the sceptics and relativists
correctly remind us, self-evident what is nature and what is con-
vention' (O'Donovan 1994: 19).

That is, there is objective morality grounded in nature, but we
know it only through revelation.[5]

Transformed by the Spirit

The Spirit enables these old-creation bodies to perform new-
creation ethics; or, in O'Donovan's terms, we have a present
anticipation of the final enjoyment through the Spirit. Without the
Spirit we are under the law:

> [I]t is the inescapable fact about anyone who confronts the deed of God,
> even the gracious deed of God, with only his own resources to respond
> to it. For man's false relation to the natural moral order is not merely a
> matter of ignorance; it is also a matter of impotence.
>
> (22)

------

5. So what of 'imposing' Christian morality on non-Christians via the state?
   O'Donovan cites, in one of his 'small print' asides, the 1966 Church of
   England document on divorce law, *Putting Asunder*, which argues that
   Christian morals cannot be imposed on secular society; the church can
   only recommend to the state self-evident moral laws. But O'Donovan
   says, 'They do not ask whether the distinction between self-evident moral
   truths and those known only to Christians corresponds to a real division
   in the truth itself or is merely a shadow cast by changing patterns of
   moral blindness' (O'Donovan 1994: 21). It is very easy, certainly, for
   Christians merely to accommodate themselves to secular perspectives in
   order to ensure they are listened to; but how far can this tactic be followed
   before Christians have nothing worth saying – or even true?

Salvation is not just the objective reality of a renewed order of things apart from myself. It is not even my knowing of that reality. No, the Spirit renews me as a moral agent. I yield myself to God's order and freely take my place within it. Thus renewal becomes subjective and eschatology is already present.

What is this renewal by the Spirit? First, it is a removal of the psychological barriers that prevent us from obeying God.

> Demands of the law merely enhanced the impotence of the subject (Rom. 7:7–13). Faced with God's summons the human will was rendered a nerveless paralytic. But the Spirit is the indwelling power of God, effecting in us both the will and the action that is according to God's good purpose (Phil. 2:13). Man is given the freedom to respond as a moral agent to what God has done for him. So far from God's intervention reducing the scope of his free will, it is the precondition for it, at least in so far as that will has to confront, not a conveniently reduced demand which it feels it can cope with, but the real challenge of the divinely created order. Only in the power of 'God who works within you to will and to do' can we respond to the command, 'Work out your own salvation'.
>
> (23)

Second, our renewal means our participation in Christ's authority within the created order – we are no longer slaves but sons. Therefore we both can and may do things now not possible before: all foods are now clean. 'Christian ethics, then, is distinguished from obedience to the law of the Old Covenant not only by its subjective moral power but by its content, because the believer shares in the authority realized in history by Christ himself' (24).

We are now able to assume our proper place assigned by God to Adam. So Christian freedom given by the Holy Spirit enables us to make moral responses creatively. We have the mind of Christ.

But this freedom does not stand isolated. We do not have freedom to overturn the objective moral order. So, third, our renewal means that the Spirit forms within us the appropriate pattern of free response to objective reality. This is love.

> [Christ's] authority over nature and his salvific concern for the true being of nature go together inseparably. And so it is that as man is given by the

Spirit to share Christ's authority, he cannot do so without love, both for
the created order in general and for the particular beings, human and
other, which stand within it in various problematic relationships . . .
Thus classical Christian descriptions of love are often found invoking
two other terms which expound its sense: the first is 'wisdom', which is
the intellectual apprehension of the order of things which discloses how
each being stands in relation to each other; the second I 'delight', which
is affective attention to something simply for *what* it is and for the fact
that it is.

(26)

We might summarize this position as (my words): having in our participation in Christ's resurrection by his Spirit been brought back
into a position where we are capable of both love and wisdom, we
are able to make moral decisions as we appropriately apply Scripture
to a properly perceived created order.

So what, then, is that created order? We are now in a position to
find out.

The objective reality of creation

O'Donovan writes, 'In proclaiming the resurrection of Christ,
then apostles proclaimed also the resurrection of mankind in
Christ; and in proclaiming the resurrection of mankind, they proclaimed the renewal of all creation with him' (31). Creation is not
merely raw material but the order in which it is composed (possibly this distinction of O'Donovan's might be found in Genesis 1 –
in the beginning God created heavens and earth formless and
empty, and spent the second lot of three days filling it.) The order
is of end and kind, teleological and generic order. Order of end is
the pattern that A is ordered to serve B, so B is A's end. Order of
kind is that A is like B, and B is like A.

The creature–creator relationship is purely teleological. But among
creatures there is a network of teleological and generic relations. For
instance, vegetables and men are both creatures, but vegetables are
ordered to men as food for their nourishment. The same is with
soil and vegetables. Some forms of generic equivalence have no

teleology; importantly the generic equivalence among men has no 'ordering to serve' within it – slavery is not natural. A more mundane example is that fish and fire are (generically) both creatures, but any further ordering is accidental or contingent.

Other categories of entities can be ordered. So operations can be ordered, as well as objects. Speech is ordered to truth, marriage to fidelity. There are many other connections like this between operations; there is no neat hierarchy (much as our scholastic tendencies might want one). That is why moral dilemmas can arise – an action that seems, in relation to one thing, compassion, is in relation to another, disloyalty.

Any thinker, Christian or not, has to decide what to do about apparent order. Is it real or illusion? If it is real, then ultimately some theological or metaphysical conclusion must be reached. If it is illusion, the illusion must be imposed by the observing mind (an empiricist position, such as advocated by David Hume).

The Christian thinks the order real. Diving and human agents both have reality and freedom, and ordered human response is to conform to the divine act. Our act of imposing order upon, or interpreting, the world, is free, precisely because it can be right or wrong. Both are possible.

Difficulties with this view

At this point O'Donovan considers some theological reservations about linking moral obligation to the natural generic–teleological order. Teleology always exists for members of a kind. Members of a kind remain so outside time and place. So if morality is tied to teleology, and teleology to generic order, morality must too transcend time and place. So if action X is good, then it is always good regardless of person, time and place. However minutely you define kind X, it remains that the moral judgment applies to the kind and not just to the particular. This causes a problem if you see morality as the demand of God's will, which must be free and unbound.

Now it is true that God was not under necessity to create the world as it is. If so, it is not creation at all but an emanation of his being: pantheism. But this proper theological concern can be fully accommodated within teleological and generic understanding of created order. Kinds might be independent of time and place, but that is by no means to make them eternally transcendent. They are merely within the temporal–spatial universe. We must resist the Platonic temptation to make universals divine.

However, the theological objection's concern for God's freedom is not limited to the initial act of creation; it also wants God's freedom to act within the universe. He must remain free to change his own order or act outside it. This means morality cannot be generic, only particular.

Now God can of course make any choice he likes, even when there is no reason to do one thing rather than another. And he treats individuals as individuals in election, not because they belong to a category. We also know he chose to act in history. He can do new things and his activity is not the same in all ages. None of this denies the existence of moral categories.

The problem with ends

There are two concerns typically raised about teleology. The first comes from science. It is virtually an axiom of modern science that there are no final causes. If it were possible to say 'X is as it is in order to serve Y', then there is little incentive to look for the material causes of the relationship between X and Y. Teleology inhibits scientific research. A second concern is the Enlightenment objection that only a free and unconditioned will imposing purposiveness on nature can be moral.

Both see the idea of 'ends' in nature as a problem. Purposiveness is exclusively a characteristic of human will. But Enlightenment thinkers, although they insisted moral judgment must be independent of teleological order in nature, still thought it had to respect generic relations (so if it is wrong to kill one man it is also wrong to kill another in the same circumstances; act without prejudice). Hume and Kant said we should act consistently in moral matters.

Now, is it possible to acknowledge generic determinations in nature without teleological ones? What makes 'humanity' a moral kind in a way that 'the upper class' is not? It requires a prior judgment as to what is of value and what is significant – a teleological judgment.

As for the science objection: science would see nature as 'an infinitely various series of possible generic equivalences' (48). So even obvious kinds are ignored in the interests of discovering new relations, or characteristics. Only by putting aside the obvious can you potentially discover the non-obvious, or at least be motivated to look for it. This is perfectly legitimate as a stratagem. But this is not to say natural teleology is false.

The proposal to see reality without ends has a similar fate. It is a useful strategy for imaginative thought, but cannot be true. For if it is, there is no such thing as a universe: no overall concept that holds it together.[6]

Also without teleology we have a dangerous misunderstanding of the place of man in the universe. It supposes the observing mind encounters an inert creation with no purpose. Scientific observation becomes the servant of usefulness. Humans take the credit for whatever order we find. We eat vegetables not because they *are* food, but because we have *devised a use* for them as food. And we are free to explore any other use we might devise for them. This is unprincipled domination, not dominion.

The history of order

Has this order always been present? Yes, but it was not fully expressed until Christ. That is because Christ is (finally) man as man was meant to be. 'He fulfils and vindicates the primal order in a way that was always implied, but which could not be realized in the fallen state of man and the universe' (54).

Redemption, then, involves both the restoration of humankind in their context as rulers of God's creation, and the restoration of creation. We don't know exactly what that will mean; we know it is

---

6. Those interested in the relationship between science and Christianity would do well to read the comments on pp. 50–52.

not just restoration to what it was before (the Garden of Eden) but to our future, originally intended, destiny. This future gives the meaning of creation. Therefore, the resurrection of Christ both redeems and transforms creation. Death is conquered. Life is given. The resurrection looks backwards and forwards.

So too Christian ethics looks backwards and forwards, to the origin and the end of the created order. It respects the natural structures of life in the world while looking forward to their transformation. It both appreciates the value of, and is aware of the failings of, worldly institutions.

In academic circles, historicism has become the preferred bestower of meaning in life. Everything has an end only in its future obsolescence. The natural exists only to be superseded: by the kingdom of heaven, by the communist paradise, by the New World Order. The value of the natural order in the present exists only as being raw material for transformation.

Now of course, O'Donovan says, we think history should be taken seriously. But that means history itself cannot be the bestower of meaning: it is a story *about* something. If not, then it is not history, but merely process.

Human participation in the renewed creation

So, to this point we have seen that there is order in creation, and it is now properly expressed in Christ. How do we, as humans, participate? O'Donovan answers, 'Morality is man's participation in the created order. Christian morality is his glad response to the deed of God which has restored, proved and fulfilled that order, making man free to conform to it' (76).

How is the order of the created universe available to our knowledge, seeing we cannot rise above it to survey it like God? Our knowledge would have to have certain characteristics:

1. It must be knowledge of things in their relations to the totality of things. We must grasp the shape of the whole even if we don't know everything about it. This is philosophy or metaphysics; having some idea of the whole and where to place

particulars within it, what meaning it gives to particulars. (We seem to have given up on the possibility of this by separation of science and religion, not to mention fragmentation of the sciences.)

2. It must be knowledge from within, as the subject participates in what he knows; for we cannot get outside totality. So science falters at the limits of the universe. This is what Qoholeth insists on (Eccl. 8:16–17).[7] Therefore, we know kinds only as an induction from particulars. But we do still know them.

3. It must be knowledge from man's position within the universe. The place of dominion is the place of knowing. Knowledge is the root of his authority over fellow-creatures and the root of the communion between humans: other parts of creation do not have knowledge as such. This means the exercise of knowledge ties up with the faithful performance of man's task, and his knowing will stand or fall with his obedience to God. Our knowledge has been inescapably compromised by rebellion. We still observe generic and teleological order, but misconstrue it and construct false world views.

4. Such knowledge must be ignorant of the end of history. This belongs to the Lord alone. We know it by revelation only, not by our knowledge of created order. But we are desperate to know it.

O'Donovan says:

> Such knowledge . . . is given to use as we participate in the life of Jesus Christ. It is the point from which the whole is discerned, 'in whom are hid all the treasures of wisdom and knowledge' (Col 2:3). He is the obedient man . . . True knowledge of the moral order is knowledge 'in Christ'.

(85)

Now, 'In Christ' does not mean ethereal. It means in the person who lived and died for us and rose. In this person alone is apprehension of the meaning of everything, and of what to do about

---

7. For an explanation of this, see my argument in Birkett 1997: 92.

it.[8] Only Christ *knows*, being the only obedient human being; so he is the only place we can go for knowledge. Everywhere else is, not total lack of knowledge, but 'misknowledge'.

For the world is broken, but it is broken *order*, not chaos. Some of it can still be known in some sense. An unbeliever need not be ignorant of the value of family, mercy, the vice of cowardice; and even unbelievers can respond. That is because we are still created to be knowers. But it will never be complete or even rightly understood knowledge. If the Creator is not known, the universe cannot be understood. It is less than partial knowledge; it is partial and misunderstood knowledge. Christ shows up this culpable 'misknowledge' for what it is.

Therefore, the Christian does not have to prove that anything worthwhile in non-Christian systems of thought had to arise from Christian influence. But neither can he or she simply embrace the perspectives of such.

Moral learning is not individual bits of knowledge to be acquired; it is an understanding of a whole order. One cannot learn 'new' moral knowledge; one can only repent of wrong understandings and change them to right. Or come to a deeper/fuller understanding of what was already true.

If a new technology or situation arises, this does not create new moral questions. Rather the created order tells us if a new development is morally significant or not.

The subjective reality

We have looked at the 'objective reality' part – Christian moral thought must respond to it. It is the reality of a world order restored in Christ. But this does not necessarily mean *we* are blessed. God could have decided to leave us out of restored creation, hopeless as we are. Or he might have decided to make us put huge effort into meeting moral standards.

---

8. That is why O'Donovan does not call it 'natural law': it is not self-evident as part of nature; it is not known naturally.

However, God did not do either of these. He gave us the Holy
Spirit, to restore us morally and make us capable of being part of a
renewed creation. Part of Christian ethics is the work of the Holy
Spirit in us: our 'subjective' reality.

> The reply of Western Christianity to [Pelagianism], a reply most influ-
> entially articulated by Augustine, is simple: there can never be a moment
> when the divine initiative pauses and waits, as it were in expectation, to
> see what man will do. Even man's 'response' is still God's initiative, and,
> so far from this undercutting the freedom of man, it is the only possible
> ground on which man can be free.

> (102)

Using the words 'objective' and 'subjective' to differentiate the
work of the Son and Spirit is useful but can be dangerous: for
example, the work of the Spirit becomes just a way of talking of
'human inwardness'. So, to be clear, O'Donovan asserts:

1. The Spirit makes the reality of redemption, which is actually
   distant from us in time, both present and authoritative.
2. The Spirit evokes our free response to this reality as moral
   agents.

The Spirit makes redemption present to us

The restoration of created order happens in the past; its universal
manifestation belongs to the future. But our whole life depends
on these two points, now. The Spirit makes God present to us *in
Christ*, because we are crucified and raised with Christ. And the
Holy Spirit makes the reality of redemption authoritative to us, for
that is how redemption comes to us. We do not just feel its after-
effects; we do not just get ready in anticipation. We *must* act. God's
action *must* be responded to. (More on this later.)

Therefore, the fact of redemption judges and recreates. It exposes the faults of the world and presents a new way. So we have
justification and sanctification, conversion and instruction, repentance and moral learning (growth). These are both aspects of the
Spirit's work, not two separate works. And of course they cannot be
temporally separated: all learning requires constant repentance. But

the distinction is still crucial. It is the distinction of death and resurrection. 'A moral authority which does not both judge and recreate
is not the authority of Christ, but a purely natural authority, to
follow which is to be conformed to the world' (105).

The Spirit evokes our free response as moral agents to the reality of redemption

He confirms and restores us as subjects of our own actions: he
enables us to act, frees us from bondage. Human willing and
working are made possible by the divine work within us (Phil.
2:13). Also the Holy Spirit enables the Christian community, the
church, to act; to act according to sin, righteousness and judgment.
This makes the life of the church possible.

The effect of the Holy Spirit on man is freedom. This makes
Christian ethics meaningful. We *can* participate in the order of creation by knowledge and action. This freedom is not inherent nor
natural: we are *set* free. This freedom is a characteristic of the
person, not his circumstances; it is potency, not possibility. Of
course there must be (at least) more than one possibility for there
to be free choice, but freedom is not the absence of limitations (as
pop philosophy has it) but the ability to choose. And the choice
can be between accepting a situation cheerfully or resentfully.
Pop philosophy is misleading in its suggestion that we maximize
freedom by maximizing possibilities. Free choice can actually
restrict freedom. For instance, many thinkers have commended
suicide as the ultimate act of inalienable freedom. But it is not an
act that affirms freedom, even if made freely. It in fact annihilates
freedom.

Freedom is a teleological structure. The end of man, from
man's point of view, is perfect liberty. We were set free in order to
be free, which is why we are *not* to use our freedom to choose sin,
which is bondage. Fallen man has freely chosen bondage, and
hates it, while not seeing what he has done. The bondage is that he
has lost touch with reality. Only the Spirit can put him back in
touch with it. And continued freedom depends upon our acting in
accord with reality, that is, morally, obediently.

Our free, engaged-with reality action, is 'obedience', 'hearing',
'attentiveness', 'hearing and doing'. The disjunction of reason and

will in Western philosophy is sin: it is precisely a separation of hearing and doing. A right-thinking human will see that to know is to will; to know the right is to will the right; to suggest a separation of these two is to allow sin. (In fact, what happens is that reason will follow will. When the will embraces sin, reason will set about creating a 'knowledge' that makes the sin permissible.)

So our restoration to reality is and must be of mind and will, knowledge and action, simultaneously. We *cannot* know reality *and* embrace sin at the same time. Conversion is repentance *and* new life.

A moral life

What, then, is the moral life? This is, O'Donovan says, a question about the fruit of the Spirit, which partly describes the moral law as it is now in Christ, and partly talks about the disposition of the moral agent.

> The counsels of prophet and apostle, then, differ by addressing polar and complementary aspects of the moral life, aspects which arise precisely from the complementary objective and subjective aspects of God's work of redemption, from his renewal of the world-order in Christ and his renewal of the moral agent by the Spirit.
>
> (183)

That is, we now have an ordered moral subject, acting in an ordered moral field.

Wisdom is the ability to see every new event as part of the permanent and ordered moral field. Wisdom perceives that every novelty somehow manifests the permanence and stability of the created order. This enables us to cope with the new and amazing. Using O'Donovan's language, the plurality of events in the world can be seen as a pluriformity: different things within a total framework of intelligibility, whose generic relationship can be understood.

So the moral agent approaches every situation with 'moral law' (i.e. wisdom regarding decisions). He holds the moral law in

thought with the particular situation; the law illuminates and inter-
prets the situation, allowing a judgment; and also leads to greater
understanding of the moral law. This applying of moral law to particular cases, casuistry, involves learning about the moral law, that
is, about the created order. Casuistry is not just a matter of solving
problems but of growing in wisdom. If we do not grow, we will
encounter situations that do not fit our understanding and our
simplistic rules will fail.

> We shall recognize suddenly that the categories of our moral under-
> standing are no longer sufficient to interpret our situation, and we
> shall reel wildly and disorderedly against them. The form which this
> rebellion takes in moral theory is the positing of random and
> meaningless 'exceptions' to moral rules . . . once we concede the
> invasion of the absurd into our moral thought . . . we have, in effect,
> abandoned our responsibilities to reality . . . The moral life will no longer
> be the consistent regard and delight elicited from us by the order of the
> real world which God has made.
>
> (195)

Not every occasion for particular judgment is also an opportunity for moral learning. Those that are, are those in which the
situation is capable of more than one description and requires an
interpretative decision: the dilemmas or quandaries where we can
understand a situation in more than one way. This is not inad-
equacy in the moral code, but arises because the moral field is
pluriform. Says O'Donovan, 'The order of reality holds together
a multitude of different kinds of moral relation, and orders
them without abolishing their differences' (199). But because it
is ultimately ordered, dilemmas will be susceptible of rational
resolution.

Codes cannot be comprehensive, because they are catalogues,
not reality itself. They are necessary for learning and organizing
knowledge. But they are not enough; it is not enough to memorize
the Ten Commandments, the Sermon on the Mount or even every
command in the Bible. Rather the Bible teaches us a comprehensive moral viewpoint: not just the bricks but how they go together.
'It is this discovery of how every area of moral responsibility is

illumined and interpreted by every other that makes the real difference between morality and legalism' (203).

We come across new situations all the time, but can deal with them because there *is* an overall order that enables us to find generic relations between the new situation and past ones. This unity also ensures the unity and integrity of the moral agent. So moral thought can talk about good or bad acts (moral field) and good or bad people (moral agents). Jesus criticized the Pharisees precisely because they concentrated on the field at the expense of the person. But it is still a tricky question as to how to correlate the two. Any such account must be such that, first, the subject's character must not be reduced to a function of his acts; and second, the subject's acts must be allowed to disclose his character, which is known only through them. 'Character is hidden from public view, while acts are open to it; but the shrewd observer will be able to read the character from the tell-tale act. For acts cannot be made entirely plausible on their own, without a character to support them' (206).

In moral theory, voluntarism tends to go with pluralism. But we can have a plurality of moral excellences without saying (for instance) that all decisions made with integrity are equally excellent. Intention does not make the choice valid. Correct moral judgment does. And the correct judgment, the thing that must be behind all moral characters, is the acknowledgment that Jesus is Lord.

Now we come to the point where O'Donovan's work comes closest to our concern: is there a clash between 'work in the world' and 'work for the kingdom'? Should these two be ordered?

Love, O'Donovan has established, is the principle that confers unifying order both upon the moral field and the character of the moral subject. 'It is the fulfilment of the moral law on the one hand, and the form of the virtues on the other' (226).

But Jesus' command is twofold: love *God*, and love your *neighbour* (Deut. 6:5; Lev. 19:18). This has led the church into problems when it sees the two as clashing: practical versus contemplative life in the Middle Ages; worship versus service, or, more recently, evangelism versus social justice.

But the two commands cannot collide if one God is the Creator. The problem is our interpretation. They are not two loves.

It is love for God that excludes all else: it takes all of heart, mind, soul and strength. I love my neighbour because before God, my neighbour and I are sharers in secondary reality, both dependent on the one who created us, and we both have the same end in him. Only in this equal dependence can I love my neighbour. I am not better than him (that would lead me to tyranny); nor worse (that would lead me to enslavement through desire or need of him). True love of neighbour requires absolute love of God, so we may see the neighbour for what he is. And pursuit of our neighbour's welfare requires seeing him, like myself, as a being whose end is in God. This does not preclude (and has not historically precluded) practical and all other kinds of help. Conversion zeal is not an 'ulterior motive', but recognition of the best good for my neighbour.

The duality of the command is still necessary because my neighbour is *not* God; love of him is a different kind from love of God. God made the other, and the other is multiple. Plurality is not fallenness (it was always there), and he wants all of them to have fellowship with each other as well as himself. A Neoplatonic seeking of God in aloneness is not Christian. Certainly prayer requires solitude, but it is in order to pray for others. Neither is seeing all humanity 'as one', or seeking to overcome individuality, Christian. We cooperate as individuals, each created by God. That is our unity.

We are taught, sometimes, to resolve potential conflict of the two commands by ordering them in terms of priority; Jesus first, others second, yourself last. Certainly in specific, practical ways we must prioritize: is money to go to this or that organization? But this is no way to think of our duties as a whole. God is always total; our duty to him always excludes all other claims. The issue is never deciding between serving God and serving others, but in which way we will serve God right now. It also obscures the fact that we can love our neighbour *only* by loving God, and our neighbour can realize the good only when he loves God.

A different way the potential conflict has been resolved is by seeing love of neighbour as the means to the end of loving God. Augustine suggested this but it has been fiercely rejected in most subsequent ethics, as we are taught to consider every individual as an end in himself, never merely a means to something else. Regardless of whether you agree, 'means' and 'ends' are inappropriate ways of understanding the relationship. They are a way of understanding deliberative planning to reach a goal; love is not a project but an appreciation of the neighbour's reality. 'We cannot love a neighbour "as a means", and neither can we love him "as an end and not a means", for means and ends are things we determine for ourselves in practical deliberation, while love is determined for us by its object' (235).

Love is ordered; love of neighbour is love of a creature who is secondary to God. But this is not demeaning of the creature, but indeed recognizing his true worth and reality. To love him for himself *is* to love him for God's sake. The ordering of love, then, is the 'free conformity of our agency to the order of things which is given in reality' (236).

The two loves, for God and neighbour, are one love, properly ordered. It is the right response to one world in multiplicity, ordered by God. But it is more than just attending to or knowing the order of reality. It is attending especially to just certain parts of reality (it excludes plants and animals) and attending in a certain way. This has led some to the (wrong) conclusion that plants and animals are less real and so we owe nothing to them. We are commanded to love only God and neighbour, not because this describes the limits of our obligations but because if we get these right, all others fall into place.

If we see the command as the most general of moral obligations, in showing the limits of what is required, then moral discourse is to work out what falls inside and outside the boundary. So, when asked 'Who is my neighbour?' (a question really asking 'Who is not my neighbour?'), Jesus' answer overturns the supposition by putting it in real, not abstract, terms. The love command is not 'respect for persons': it is 'helping others wherever and whenever you come across them'.

Many activities of the church (teaching, evangelizing, acts of service etc.) are good things to do. Faith and hope look forward to the end; indeed without their objects they are less than pointless. Living a moral life is like faith and hope. It is love, which is unintelligible except as a participation in the love of God, participating in the end times. 'The conviction of a final triumph of God's will, in which every other created will is conformed to it, makes sense of our present relative and imperfect commitment to doing God's will' (247).

Does love have a reward? This claim has typically been met with two kinds of objections: that there cannot be another, greater good than love itself; and that if we are motivated by reward, we are not truly loving. O'Donovan's answers to these objections are typically profound. First, he answers, there is no greater good than love; but the reward is not a 'higher' good, just more of the same thing, a renewal and perfection of the good we already have. To the second objection, he answers that to deny future glory may sound noble but actually detaches morality from reality. Love implies a desire for the good to be actualized, which means yearning for the new creation; the fact that I know it will also be good for me does not deny the truth and properness of that desire.

Living in Christ

Jesus concentrates on where a life finishes, not where it went along the way. The last moment of the thief on the cross's life shaped the whole of his life, when he encountered and recognized reality. Properly seen, this is, O'Donovan says, not a last-minute decision to repent, but a very late encounter with the reality that would have changed his life at any time. This encounter creates love and is crucial to morality, much more than disposition or human character. And we know the final meaning of our lives not through introspection, but through faith in the objective word of God, which keeps on turning us to reality. In this way, baptism is what assures us of the redemptive presence of Christ, because it reminds us of his objective act; nothing about the person, his good acts, changed character or appearance of certainty, can give that assurance.

The shape of a human life is decisively established by the moment of encounter with Christ. Yes, virtue is better than vice, but in itself it does not tell us what it means for eternity. The question is whether this life (or act or character) belongs to the renewed and transformed world, and the answer can be, only in terms of the relation to Christ. We do have opposites in Christianity: the broad way, the narrow way, love/sin and so on. But in the light of the end, even the most complex issues of morality become simple.

The difficulty is that when moral thought loses contact with eschatology but retains the ultimate dualism of good and evil (which is still true), it becomes legalism. It attempts to make the codified law entirely comprehensive. It makes every decision a choice between obeying or disobeying God's law. The fate of the soul rests on every moral decision; this leads to great scrupulousness, and lack of gospel freedom.

As O'Donovan concludes:

> The ultimate and simple decision is not found in the books of human deeds, but in the book of life, where it is a question of Yes or No: either a name is there, or it is not. But the book of life does not supplant the books of men's deeds; rather, those books, when read in the light of that book, take on the character of a correspondingly simple and final decision, a Yes or No to God's grace.
>
> (264)

We have a decision to make at every point; to love or not to love. But this is only possible, and only finally worth doing, because of God's grace in Christ.

Some thoughts on new living in an old creation

We live for the future and our lives are shaped by it, but since we are still living here, how do we solve the moral problems that arise every day, mostly because of living in a fallen world?

Whether the new creation is this one with frustration removed, or a totally new one from nothing, it is going to be radically different. There will be no marriage; how can we imagine that? Family has been the fundamental social unit for the whole of human existence, the only one we know. What would it be like without it? Marriage is the context for bringing up godly children. Does this mean there will be no children in the new creation? How can that be? It is unimaginably different. Not to mention the other curiosities: for the glorified believer, no suffering, no tears. No food chain? No predator–prey relationships? How will ecological balance be maintained? How different will animals be with a totally changed chemistry and physiology?

Is evangelism more important than secular work? Of course it is. Evangelism has the potential to save someone for an eternity of praising God. It is the absolutely most loving thing you can do for God and for your neighbour. The overriding factor is not creation ethics nor kingdom ethics, but love. For any decision, what is the most loving thing I can do towards God and my neighbour?

So there are not two classes of Christians; there is one: those who love. But there is still a ranking of things we might devote our lives to. The most loving thing we can ever do for another person is help them to know Christ. Every Christian must consider how they can do this, and whether they can do it more. That does not make anything else pointless. We are called upon to love whole-heartedly.

Can one person do everything that is loving towards all humans? No; and we are not asked to. God gives the church different gifts to fulfil the different needs there are to build the church: build it upward in maturity, and outward in bringing in members. God gives some to be evangelists, some to be teachers, some to be Christian politicians, some to be newspaper columnists, some to be rubbish collectors (which is of great usefulness to many people – we must not be middle-class in our loving!).

But every Christian individually must live for the sake of loving our neighbour, in whatever capacity we may. And the greatest act of love possible is to bring people to knowledge of the greatest act of love ever: Christ's death and resurrection for the salvation of many.

3. SAMUEL RUTHERFORD AND THE CONFESSIONALLY CHRISTIAN STATE

David Field

Evangelical defeatism and public theology

'Even a loser can win when he's up against a defeatist' (Steyn 2007: no p.). Islam is definitely a loser and humanism is definitely a loser. But sadly, when it comes to matters of public theology, most evangelicals are defeatists.

It is remarkable, really, that evangelicals should be defeatists, a dreadful failure of perspective that comes from a refusal to look up. Our discussions are sometimes like a debate between the two men in Slough that has been going on for the last 120 years. One of them insists that humans cannot fly, that if God had intended us to fly he would have given us wings: we know the arguments. The other has produced detailed documents showing how, if pedal speed can be maintained to power the mechanical wings, it is scientifically possible for humans to fly almost a mile. Meantime, a huge passenger jet containing between 300 and 600 people passes overhead every two minutes.

Evangelical defeatism is a failure of biblical perspective. After all, the risen Lord Jesus has been given all authority in heaven and

on earth and has been made head over all things for the church; he
is the ruler of the kings of the earth and is putting his enemies
beneath his feet; he has presumably asked the Father for the
nations as his inheritance and the ends of the earth as his possession – and so he will receive them. All nations will bow to Jesus
and all kings will serve him, and his kingdom will grow to become
the largest plant in the garden with the nation-birds finding rest in
its branches. His kingdom is the stone in Daniel 2 that crushed the
kingdoms of men and is growing to become a mountain-empire
that fills the whole earth. He is the firstborn from among the dead
and therefore it is right that in all things he has the first place. He
has been highly exalted and not only *will* every knee bow to him
but every knee *should* bow to him.

Evangelical defeatism is a failure of historical perspective. After
all, the statistics are out there. It took 1,400 years for 1% of the
world's population to become Christians, and then another 360
years for that to double to 2%. Another 170 years saw that grow
from 2% to 4%, and then between 1960 and 1990 the proportion
of the world's population made up of Bible-believing Christians
rose from 4% to 8%. Now, in 2007, a third of the world's population confesses that Jesus is Lord and 11% of the world's
population comprises 'evangelical' Christians. The evangelical
church is growing twice as fast as Islam and three times as fast
as the world's population. South America is turning Protestant
faster than Continental Europe did in the sixteenth century. South
Koreans reckon that they can evangelize the whole of North
Korea within five years once that country opens up. And then
there's the Chinese church, consisting of tens of millions of
Christians who have learned to pray, who have confidence in
Scripture, who know about spiritual warfare, have been schooled
in suffering and are qualified to rule. One day in the next century
that church (tens of millions of Christians trained to die) will be
released into global mission and our prayers for the fall of Islam
will be answered.

Evangelical defeatism in matters of public theology is a failure
of biblical and historical perspective. Lacking that perspective,
British evangelical defeatists are riddled with white and Christian
guilt and are marked by parochial and pessimistic self-loathing and

suspicion. They offer their hands to the humanists' handcuffs and their children to their indoctrination centres, making loud assurances that the last thing they would want to do would be to 'impose their morality' on others. In public policy debates they speak in the name of the 'whole person' and 'faith perspectives' rather than in the name of King Jesus. In their Bible studies they have hermeneutical fits if someone suggests that the Old Testament might be relevant for our discussions of public theology, insisting rather that Christians are the wilderness community who live under the cross, are marked by suffering and are destined for political and cultural impotence. Evangelical defeatists begin to twitch if someone mentions too loudly in public that the Bible is God's infallible and sufficient Word, that Blair and Brown and Cameron and the rest of them are idolatrous high priests of the greatest false god of modern times, the state, and will one day be on their knees before King Jesus, and that the task the Lord Jesus Christ has given the church is to subdue the earth and fill it, that is, disciple the nations.

Samuel Rutherford and his fellow-believers in the Covenanting tradition of the seventeenth century must look down from heaven in disbelief. Their gospel confidence and robust theocratic and 'Christendomite' vision produced an understanding of 'public theology' that honoured the kingship of Jesus and, under scrutiny, proves a good deal more consistent and durable than alternative proposals adopted by many Christians today. Rutherford's writing implies what might be called a 'confessionally Christian state', and this chapter aims to describe and evaluate this in comparison with the three available options for the constitutional arrangement of a nation state.

Samuel Rutherford's *Lex, rex*

First published in 1644, Samuel Rutherford's *Lex, rex* (Rutherford 1644)[1] is one of the fifty most important works of public theology

---

1. The original 1644 edition is held by the British Library, the Bodleian, and
   by the University libraries of Cambridge, Glasgow, Edinburgh, Aberdeen,

yet to have been written.[2] Charles II hated it and had it burned at
the Restoration, but it was acclaimed by its intended audience in
the 1640s: John Coffey says:

> According to the Scottish moderate, Henry Guthry, every member
> of the 1645 General Assembly 'had in his hand that Book lately
> published by Mr Samuel Rutherford . . . [which was] so idolised
> that whereas Buchanan's treatise *De Jure Regni apud Scotos*, was looked
> upon as an oracle, this coming forth, it was slighted (as not
> anti-monarchical enough) and Rutherford's *Lex, rex* only thought
> authentic'.
>
> (Coffey 1997: 151)

Coffey goes on to describe the book as 'an unusually comprehensive statement of Calvinistic political thought' and this being the
case, as conservative evangelical and Reformed Christians in this
country recover a biblical interest in public theology, study of
Rutherford's work may well prove to be a worthwhile exercise,
not least because the assumptions, substance and implications
of his arguments in defence of armed resistance against the
tyrant amount to a forceful case for what we might call 'the

Footnote 1 (*cont.*)

> Nottingham, and the London School of Economics. An 1843 edition
> has been reprinted a number of times since the 1970s and *Lex, rex* is also
> to be found online at http://www.constitution.org/sr/lexrex.htm, and
> in a fully searchable digital edition with modern orthography at
> http://www.lonang.com/exlibris/rutherford/index.html. For a thor-
> ough exposition of Rutherford's *Lex, rex*, with extensive bibliographical
> leads, see my 'Put not your Trust in Princes: Samuel Rutherford, the
> Four Causes, and the Limitation of Civil Government', in Clark 2005:
> 83–151.

2. I have put online 'The Reduced *Lex, rex*', a 44-page pdf document listing
   available editions of Rutherford's book, giving the full title page and the
   detailed table of contents and providing selected illustrative quotations
   that give a flavour of the whole work. It can be seen at
   http://www.davidpfield.com/other/Reduced-Lex-rex.pdf.

confessionally Christian state' or, in honour of Rutherford, the 'covenanted nation'.[3]

Five years later, Rutherford published another work of public theology, *A Free Disputation against Pretended Liberty of Conscience*. This is not the sort of title that commends itself to many people these days and these two works of Rutherford together seem to confirm what many modern evangelicals suspect, namely that belief in a confessional state produces, or at the least tends to, a fundamental intolerance.

Actually the opposite is true, as there are only three possibilities. The first is a *false confession*, which is idolatrous because it makes a false god to be the ultimate authority. The second is *no confession*, which is tyrannical because it means that the actions of the state are ungrounded. The third is a *Christian confession*, which is the foundation of justice and true tolerance, better called 'liberty'. Some Christians, so-called principled pluralists, try to find a fourth position but, as we will see later, this position is unstable and resolves, under pressure, into one of the other three positions.

In the mid-1630s Charles I and Archbishop Laud sought to impose religious uniformity upon the Scottish Church, and, when this was resisted, raised an army to march against the Scots. In 1642, when the Scots refused to give in to any more of the English Parliament's demands for constitutional and ecclesiastical reform, Charles raised the Royal Standard in Nottingham and the English Civil War began. In 1643, the Scots made an alliance with the English Parliament, providing military support in exchange for further commitments to reform of the English Church.

Lex, rex is a defence of the Scots' military action against Charles, both in the so-called Bishops' Wars of 1639–40 and, from 1643 onwards, in support of the Parliamentary side in the English Civil War.

---

3. Supporting the claim that England is such a covenanted nation, see *The Form and Order of Service . . . Observed in The Coronation of Her Majesty Queen Elizabeth II . . . 1953* <http://www.oremus.org/liturgy/coronation/index.html> (accessed 8 Sept. 2007).

The first sentence of *Lex, rex* outlines the subject matter of the book. Rutherford simply states, 'I reduce all that I am to speak of the power of kings, to the author or efficient, – the matter or subject, – the form or power, – the end and fruit of their government, – and to some cases of resistance' (Rutherford 1644: 1).

Rutherford is working with the four *aitia* of Aristotle, often referred to as the four 'causes': the *efficient* cause, the *material* cause, the *formal* cause and the *final* cause. In his 'cases of resistance' he discusses the grounds, occasions and manner of restraining, restricting or withdrawing the king's power, and this discussion flows from what he has said about the four causes.

If we reorder the causes (to final, efficient, formal and material) and take 'cases of resistance' to be 'forms of limitation', we may rephrase the conclusions of *Lex, rex* as a series of questions: 'What is the purpose or goal of government? Who or what brings government into being? What is it that makes government government, or what is the essence of government? What is government made out of? What are the due limitations of civil government?'

By way of further clarification, it should be noted that Rutherford's work was written in reply to an earlier work by John Maxwell, the former Bishop of Ross and in the 1640s a chaplain to Charles I. Maxwell had written a book entitled *The Sacred and Royal Prerogative of Christian Kings*, whereas Rutherford's title continues, *The Law and the Prince. A Dispute for the Just Prerogative of King and People*. To caricature in order to clarify, Maxwell argues, 'God has appointed kings, the word of the king is law and no resistance against kings can be justified.' Rutherford responds, 'God has appointed kings as agents and servants of his law for the good of the people and thus, when they act contrary to God's law and the good of the people, they may be resisted.' Is the king over the law or is the law over the king?

The main lines of Rutherford's argument may be stated briefly as follows:

1. The *final cause* of government: *what is its purpose?* The purpose of civil government is to secure the well-being of the people by protecting them and the church so that they may attain their

highest good in the knowledge of God in Christ. This is *why* government exists.

2. The *efficient cause* of government: *who or what brings it into being?* The God who rules all things through his exalted Son brings government into being using the consent of the people as a means. God is the primary cause and the people are the secondary cause; God is the principal and the people are the agent. This is *how* government comes to be.

3. The *formal cause* of government: *what is the essence of government?* What makes government *government* is its submission to and embodiment of the law of God discovered through study and application of his infallible and sufficient Word, the Bible. Embodiment of the law of God: this is what government is.

4. The *material cause* of government: *what is the stuff out of which government is made?* Government is made of ordinary sinful human beings, equal with all others by nature and each of whom is directly accountable in conscience and on Judgment Day to the one true living God. This is what government is *made out of.*

Rutherford's defence of armed resistance against the tyrant follows from each of these points. Combining the first two points, we may say that if government works against its purpose, then those whom God used to put it in power may resist its abuse of power or put it out of power. Combining the third and fourth points, we may say that if government ceases to be government, then those in places of government have removed their own crowns and are nothing more than sinful humans and the people are obliged neither to fall in with the sins of such false rulers nor to attribute any more legitimacy to their attacks than they would to the attacks of any other sinners.

Lex, rex and the confessionally Christian state

Although Rutherford's questions were not the same as ours, nevertheless, when we do bring some of *our* questions to *Lex, rex*, we find that in this astonishing work of 'public theology' Rutherford has constructed for us a platform for the confessional state, the

Christian nation, the establishment of Christianity, the covenanted
nation or Christendom.

Illustratively those who want a confessional state, a Christian
nation, the establishment of Christianity, and who seek the coming
of Christendom could be identified as those who assert:

> The first line of the constitution of each and every nation on earth
> should include a statement such as 'The triune God, Father, Son, and
> Holy Spirit, is the one true living God and he is the maker, ruler,
> redeemer, and judge of the world. The Bible is his infallible and
> altogether authoritative Word. Jesus Christ, the Son of God, is King of
> Kings and Lord of lords and has all authority in heaven and on earth.'[4]

---

4. Although flawed in various ways, it may be of interest to include
here four articles from *The Instrument of Government* (1654)
<http://www.olivercromwell.org/protectorate/protectorate_6.htm>
(accessed 8 Sept. 2007). This could be regarded as England's first written
constitution.

'XVII. That the persons who shall be elected to serve in Parliament,
shall be such (and no other than such) as are persons of known integrity,
fearing God, and of good conversation, and being of the age of twenty-
one years.

'XXXV. That the Christian religion, as contained in the Scriptures, be
held forth and recommended as the public profession of these nations;
and that, as soon as may be, a provision, less subject to scruple and contention, and more certain than the present, be made for the
encouragement and maintenance of able and painful teachers, for the
instructing the people, and for discovery and confutation of error, hereby,
and whatever is contrary to sound doctrine; and until such provision be
made, the present maintenance shall not be taken away or impeached.

'XXXVI. That to the public profession held forth none shall be com-
pelled by penalties or otherwise; but that endeavours be used to win them
by sound doctrine and the example of a good conversation.

'XXXVII. That such as profess faith in God by Jesus Christ (though
differing in judgment from the doctrine, worship or discipline publicly
held forth) shall not be restrained from, but shall be protected in, the profession of the faith and exercise of their religion; so as they abuse not this

Rutherford would have regarded such a thing as perfectly obvious and a few moments reflecting on his arguments in *Lex, rex* shows as much. Each of his four main points requires acknowledgment of the one true living triune God, Father, Son and Holy Spirit. It is the *will of God* through the consent of the people that brings about government's existence, the *law of God* that defines government's essence, the *creatures of God* that form government's raw materials, and the *purpose of God* that provides government's *raison d'être*. Without an acknowledgment of God, all of Rutherford's claims about government are evacuated of content. Take away the confession of the true God and there is nothing left. The presupposition, content and implication of *Lex, rex* is that the public and political confession of the one true living God, Father, Son and Holy Spirit, is the only sufficient, coherent and durable foundation for the state, and the submissive and explicit acknowledgment of God is necessary to the faithful and effective conduct of government.

In summary, then, Samuel Rutherford's arguments in *Lex, rex* are intended to provide a defence of taking up arms against the tyrant and are founded upon an exposition of the purpose, origin, nature and raw materials of civil government. That same exposition also shows how Rutherford would straightforwardly be a supporter of what might be called the covenanted Christian nation, or the confessional state.

Three questions may be asked about the relationship between the lordship of Jesus and the kings of the earth:

1. Is Jesus Christ the ruler of the kings of the earth?
2. Is it desirable that the kings of the earth should acknowledge this?
3. Is it desirable that the kings of the earth qua kings should publicly confess this?

---

liberty to the civil injury of others and to the actual disturbance of the public peace on their parts: provided this liberty be not extended to Popery or Prelacy, nor to such as, under the profession of Christ, hold forth and practise licentiousness.'

Non-Christians and Christians are, of course, distinguished by their answers to the first two questions, but those who support and those who oppose the Christian confessional state are distinguished by their answer to the third. Rutherford and the covenanting tradition answer the third question with no less a ringing and confident 'yes' than they give to the first two.

Given the purpose, origin, nature and stuff of the human person, it is clear and important that each human being confess the triune God, recognize Jesus as Lord, and live with the Word of God as his or her supreme authority. To Rutherford and the covenanting tradition it is no less clear and important, given the purpose, origin, nature and stuff of human government, that each human ruler also confess the triune God, recognize Jesus as Lord and live with the Word of God as his or her supreme authority.

Sixteen objections to the confessionally Christian state

For all this, however, there are few things better able to raise evangelical hackles than the idea of the confessional state. A number of important objections are frequently brought and my intention in this section is to state some of the more common objections and to channel a Rutherfordian response.

A constitution may be thought of as *Pears Cyclopaedia* defines it: 'the fundamental organic law or principles of government of a nation, state, society, or other organisation, embodied in written documents, or implied in the institutions and customs of the country or society' (Cook 2004: L.26). And it will be recalled that, illustratively, those who support the confessional state believe it to be a biblically required and important goal that the first line of the constitution of each and every nation on earth should include a statement such as 'The triune God, Father, Son and Holy Spirit, is the one true living God and he is the maker, ruler, redeemer and judge of the world. The Bible is his infallible and altogether authoritative Word. Jesus Christ, the Son of God is King of kings and Lord of lords and has all authority in heaven and on earth.'

Objection 1: This is a departure from New Testament priorities and from the New Testament agenda for the church. This objection falsely assumes that to regard something not explicitly described as a Christian objective in the New Testament as desirable is to depart from the New Testament priorities and agenda. But it is possible to believe that it would be a good and proper thing for the nations of the world to have explicitly Christian constitutions without thereby implying that the achievement of that end demands a particular type or degree of activity from particular people or institutions.

Christian constitutionalists make no claim that the institutional church should divert resources or give a certain amount of attention to the establishment of a Christian constitution. The validity of the objection depends entirely upon what priority and attention is given to the matter. If proponents of the confessional state suggested that achieving constitutional change should be our top priority and that we should divert all our Christian energy to it, then this would be a fair objection. If, on the other hand, the suggestion was simply that this is how the world would look if all was as it should be, then it is being used as a critical standpoint and as a legitimate prayer goal. In that case, it would be like saying, 'We seek a world in which there are no abortions and in which no one dies by starvation.' Most Christians would agree that that is a biblically required state of affairs (it is an expression of the revealed will of God) and yet such agreement says nothing about how much energy and attention should be given to bringing it about.

And just as Oliver O' Donovan speaks of Christendom as a *response* to mission rather than an alternative to or a distraction from it (O'Donovan 1996: 195), so, it must be asked, what if the civil magistrate is converted? Imagine that the church is faithful in mission and that, through the blessing of God upon that faithfulness, one day Parliament comes to the church with this appeal: 'We know that Jesus Christ is king of kings and that we must give account to him for all our actions. We know that in our capacity as rulers we are to acknowledge the supreme authority of Jesus. We know that the Bible is sufficient to equip us for every good work. And we have been asked by the people of this country to provide a written constitution. Please, O Church, while we are not for a moment relinquishing to you our God-given responsibility to rule, we would like you to help us understand what the Bible teaches on

this matter.' That the proponent of the confessional state at that
point has an answer to give to Parliament says nothing whatever
about whether or not he has departed from the priorities and
agenda of the New Testament. Indeed failure to have an answer is
a sign of unfaithfulness.

This in turn relates to the need to understand our times.
Ministers of the Word of God would have less to say about
national constitutions in Athens and Corinth in the middle of the
first century than they would in Edinburgh or London in the
middle of the seventeenth century or than they will in Chile and
China in the middle of the twenty-second century. Purely in terms
of covenantal context, Samuel Rutherford's address to the powers
in the middle of the seventeenth century may be more like
the setting of an Old Testament prophet than that of a New
Testament evangelist because, after all, Rutherford was facing a
nation characterized by almost universal profession of faith in the
true God and by the failure to live consistently with that profession of faith.

All of this is simply to say that believing that it would be a good
and proper thing for the nations of the world to have explicitly
Christian constitutions says nothing at all about the priority a
person assigns to it. Most Christians would regard a litter-free and
a slavery-free world as desirable, but unless they go on to demand
certain types or levels of activity we would not accuse them of
departing from priorities and the agenda of the New Testament.
I personally believe that the world would be more closely conformed to the revealed will of God if all churches used alcoholic
wine for the Lord's Supper and if we returned to the gold standard, but that says nothing about whether or not I am faithful to the
priorities and agenda of the New Testament.

Objection 2: This amounts to the worship of 'power'. It is
indeed possible that proponents of the confessional state may
be lured by the attraction of the 'power' of writing constitutions.
They may fall into the temptation of thinking that if only they had
their hands on political power, then all would be well. But this
objection resolves down into two forms.

The first form, which some anabaptists might be attracted to,
amounts to saying that all political power is corrupt and corrupting

and is, as such, to be avoided and resisted. The problem with this is both that it fails to recognize the strong biblical possibility that the righteous may be given positions of rule and, much more importantly, that it cedes the concept of 'power' to the unrighteous. If the life, teaching and death of Jesus have shown us that leadership is a form of service, and that power may be exercised in humility in order to bless others, then to resist or run from holding power as intrinsically and unavoidably corrupt and corrupting is to deny Christ. If all exercise of authority is proud and violent, then why do we love Jesus so much, since he has, and exercises, *all* authority in heaven and on earth? The stance of radically egalitarian, pacifist, non-resistance proves too much: eschewing all exercise of 'power' leaves no room for activities with explicit biblical mandate such as the expulsion of false teachers, the discipline of children, the punishment of criminals, and the judgment of Satan.

The second form of this objection to the confessional state (that it amounts to the worship of power) is simply an (entirely appropriate) alert to the dangers of power and to the temptation to thinking that writing a constitution could take the place of or bring about the changing of human persons. But this danger is common to all those who believe that political power is not intrinsically evil and constitutes as much an argument against opponents of the confessional state as against proponents of it. In that sense, it is strictly irrelevant.

Objection 3: This will lead to the adoption of unbiblical methods of societal change. This objection is similarly strictly irrelevant. Yes, it is possible that proponents of the confessional state might place too much hope in the attainment of that goal or might seek to achieve it by unbiblical means, but there is nothing about holding the goal that makes this necessarily true nor anything about not holding this goal that makes a person less susceptible to adopting unbiblical methods of societal change. Evangelical proponents of the confessional state rightly stress the non-violent, multigenerational, servant-minded, prayerful and loving preaching and living of the gospel in the power of the Spirit as the means of societal change. Pure worship, living as the alternative society, serving and praying and witnessing, and witnessing and praying and serving are the ways the gospel advances. By

definition, no *evangelical* supporter of the idea of the confessional
state could believe that this required retreating from the priorities
of gospel preaching and godly living just as he would assert that
there is no reason why affirming and living those priorities
required the abandonment of the desire that Christ be given first
place in all things, including the constitutions of nations.

**Objection 4: The confessionally Christian state has no room
for democracy or tolerance: it imposes belief on people.** All law is
imposed morality and the real questions, therefore, are whether
the morality is God-given and whether the laws are just. But it is
worth noting how Rutherford's explanation of the efficient cause
of government precisely answers the charge that the confessional
state is anti-democratic. He insists that while God is the principal
efficient cause of government, the consent of the people is necessary for the legitimacy of government (though he believes that
there are other ways of giving that consent than through democrat-
ic ballot). That, then, being the case, for a government to impose a
confession on the state without the consent of the people itself
delegitimizes the government. The basis upon which a Christian
confession for the state rests itself rules out the imposition of
such a confession without the consent of the people.

We have no difficulty in understanding this in relation to individuals and the gospel. While it is true that all people *should*
personally acknowledge the lordship of Jesus and while it is desirable that they do so, some methods of bringing about such a state
of affairs are forbidden by the gospel itself. Similarly while it is true
that all nations *should* constitutionally acknowledge the lordship of
Jesus and while it is desirable that they do so, some methods of
bringing about such a state of affairs are forbidden by the gospel
itself. What is so difficult about that?

Objection 5: The confessional state has a bad track record. At
this point most Christians have Constantine and the Crusades,
Calvin's Geneva and Cromwell's Protectorate in mind.[5] Significant

---

5. Most British evangelical defeatist Christians, that is! See Jenkins 2006 for
   evidence that the African church is a lot less troubled by the political conquest and claims of Jesus.

defences can be mounted against the charges usually brought, but there is no need to mount such defences: a bad track record is not itself a compelling argument. For the first few days of trying to walk, a year-old boy may have a bad track record consisting of hurting himself, repeatedly failing, and damaging things around him. And yet most parents do not, after a few days, conclude, 'He's obviously not meant to be a walker – don't let him do it: he'll only hurt himself and others.' So what if the infant church (in these early days of the first couple of millennia since the resurrection) has notched up a few embarrassing and premature and painful failures? Non-confessional states are hardly marked by justice and liberty for all, by non-aggression, administrative competence, non-intrusiveness and harm-free righteousness. How is the track record of non-Christian confessional states such as Muslim states and Marxist states? How is the track record of liberal democracies keen to spread liberal democracy into the Middle East in order to bring about regional security and engage in nation-building? The self-loathing of evangelical Christians in the West that has allowed the humanists to intimidate us with a few mentions of past failures is ridiculous: 'Oh, I love Jesus, I believe the Bible is true, so please, please don't put political power in my hands because I might misuse it. Don't let me near government. Please give political power to the Jesus-haters and the Bible-despisers. Give it to the Muslims and the atheists and the humanists: they will be so much better at ruling wisely and righteously than we could be!'

Objection 6: This goal is associated with a coercive, arrogant and intolerant demeanour. The desire for a confessional Christian state is associated with a triumphalist, arrogant and intolerant demeanour. Another strictly irrelevant argument. After all, conservative evangelicalicalism is *associated* with a narrow, bigoted and proud demeanour. Sadly the association is on occasion rightly made, but as conservative evangelicals are rightly quick to answer, this is in spite of, and not a necessary consequence of, being a conservative evangelical.

Objection 7: We cannot confidently hold this as a goal until we have solved hermeneutical problems about the Christian use of the Old Testament. Why not? Are not some things already perfectly clear? It is clear that the Old Testament is God-breathed,

useful for teaching, reproof, correction and training in righteousness; that the Old Testament points to Christ and equips us for
every good work; that the Old Testament contains wise, just and
beautiful laws which expressed God's character and purposes for
one particular social order once upon a time. There is nothing
about the desire for a written constitution acknowledging Father,
Son and Holy Spirit as the one true living God, recognizing the
Bible as God's perfect word and the Lord Jesus Christ as the one
to whom all authority in heaven and on earth has been given that
requires all of our hermeneutical problems to be solved before we
acknowledge the legitimacy of that desire. In any case, the way that
the Lord brings his church to maturity is not by first getting everything clear in their minds and then telling them to proceed to
action. Rather it is as his people are faithful and attempt obedience
with some knowledge that the Lord reveals more to them. God
has not ordered the world so that persons first arrive at adult
understanding and then begin to live; rather persons begin to live
on the basis of true, though childlike, understanding, and then
grow in understanding *as* they live in obedience.

    **Objection 8: Proponents of a confessionally Christian state
fail fully to take into account our fallibility and ignorance. Other
voices must be heard.** To repeat an earlier answer, we do know
some things rather clearly: the triune God is maker, ruler and judge
of all things; Jesus has all authority in heaven and on earth; the
Bible is the infallible and sufficient Word of God; and civil government is God's servant, an avenger of his wrath on the evil-doer. In
relation to those big and clear things, there is no command from
God to listen to other voices. Adam and Eve, ignorant and fallible
as they were, were not obliged thereby to give the serpent a hearing,
were they? And the people of God addressed in Deuteronomy 13,
even though they were fallible and ignorant, were forbidden by
God himself to give a hearing to the idolater.

    If there were never closure, judgment or decision until all voices
were one, then there would be no laws or punishments at all
because we have no reason to believe that Satan is likely to give up
his dissent. If we pass judgments or make decisions while there are
still dissenting voices, then we have rightly concluded that there
are some things that our ignorance and fallibility do not prevent us

acting on. If we wait to act until we are omniscient and infallible, then we will never act, but if we live by the Word of the omniscient and infallible God, then we find ourselves animated rather than paralysed.

Objection 9: The desire for a confessionally Christian state represents an over-realized eschatology. As mentioned above, it is possible (indeed necessary) to state what is desirable in the light of God's revealed will without predicting that this will be actualized before the return of the Lord Jesus Christ. In the case of the individual, entire personal Christlikeness is desirable. Does the fact that this will not be attained before resurrection morning mean that in thinking about it, praying for it, and wishing to move towards it, I am guilty of over-realized eschatology? Not at all. In fact, if I had no idea what Christlikeness looked like, then I would have neither a measure of my current faithfulness or unfaithfulness; nor would I have a goal to aspire to. A proper description of the standard becomes the (within-history) unattainable but nevertheless desired and striven-for goal and the measure of current faithfulness.

And so it is that we want kings to bow down to Christ and nations to serve him; we want the nations streaming to Zion to learn the law of the Lord; we hope that the kings will be wise and the rulers instructed, and that they will serve the Lord with fear, and honour the Son; we look forward to the growing empire of the Lord welcoming the bird-nations into its branches; to seeing the nations themselves subdued and discipled by the gospel. None of us knows how far these things will be actualized before the return of Christ. All of us know that they will not be fully actualized before then. But far from the mere desire for these things amounting to over-realized eschatology, in fact, the absence of a desire for these things means that we have neither a critical standpoint against which to measure the present nor a righteous aspiration as we move into the future.

Objection 10: This is an unbiblical confusion of authorities: it leads to ecclesiocracy. The Bible teaches what might be called 'institutional pluralism and ethical monism'. That is, there are multiple governments but only one ultimate Lord. Church government is accountable to the Lord Jesus Christ; civil government is accountable to the Lord Jesus Christ; family government is accountable to the Lord Jesus Christ. This does not, however, mean that the church rules the state nor that the state rules the church. A confessional Christian state is merely telling the truth about civil government, namely that it is established by God and accountable to him, and that it is to be ruled by his Word. The goal of a Christian constitution, far from being a confusion of authorities, is a recognition of the overarching authority over all earthly authorities: that of the Lord Jesus Christ.

Objection 11: It's too late: we live in a post-Christian world. This objection requires knowledge of the date of Christ's return, which Jesus has told us we do not have. How long will it be before we see our blessed hope, the manifestation of the glory of our great God and Saviour Jesus Christ? What if the Lord were to show his steadfast love to thousands of generations? What if, here in 2007, we are still in the early church? What if, far from taking a 'long' time (four thousand years) after the fall to send the Redeemer, when we reach Judgment Day we will look back and say, 'almost as soon as Adam fell (in just four thousand years) God sent his Son'?

Global perspective as well as temporal perspective is needed. Christians in Africa, South America and south-east Asia would be surprised to hear talk of a 'post-Christian world' or of it being too late for the establishment of confessionally Christian nations. We do not live in a post-Christian world; we live in an anti-Christian phase in the West.

Objection 12: The establishment of Christian national constitutions is too difficult and, in any case, perfectionist. To repeat what was said above, entire personal Christlikeness before seeing Jesus face to face is also 'too difficult', but this does not mean that it is not to be our legitimate direction of travel. Walking is 'too difficult' for three-month-old children and yet just a year later most of them are doing it. Christ is King, his Spirit is omnipotent, grace is stronger than sin and perhaps the people of God need more of the grace of patience: confidence that stops measuring things by the rule of single locations and single lifetimes and looks up and around to the advance of the gospel over many generations and across the nations.

Objection 13: This is no different from a Muslim arguing for **Sharia** *law.* This will be addressed in more detail below, but it should be noted that this objection is founded upon a sort of 'moral equivalence' argument that unnecessarily troubles many Christians who have been indoctrinated by the state and morally fashioned by the humanist media into self-suspicion and moral timidity. The form of the argument leads to the idea that blessing and cursing are very little different because they both involve speaking words; or that poison and medicine are very little different because they both come in little white powders; or that racism and stopping at red traffic lights are very little different because they both involve acting on the basis of colour discrimination. The fact that there are some structural similarities between Christian commitment to the confessional state and Muslim commitment to the confessional state does not mean that they are not diametrically opposed to one another: one is founded upon the righteous recognition of the truth that Jesus is Lord and the other upon wicked adherence to the lie that there is one God, Allah, and that Muhammad is his prophet.

This is the line of argument which tells us that doctrinal discrimination is the Inquisition, that prison is slavery and that loving corporal discipline is violent abuse. Christians 'sound like' Muslim fundamentalists when they say, 'God is great,' or when they say, 'The true God is the source of everything good and must be obeyed in every detail of life,' but this is no cause for alarm. Christians 'look like' Muslim fundamentalists when they have two eyes, a nose and a mouth. In response, it could be claimed that some Christians 'sound like' atheist humanists and liberal statists when they insist that religion in the public square is a dangerous thing. But the argument itself is flawed: similarity of form must not be confused with identity of substance.

Objection 14: Pluralistic liberal democracy works fine. It will be shown below that liberal democracy is intrinsically tyrannical but it is a fact that some people living under liberal democracies have enjoyed relatively stable and comfortable social and political experiences. We need to note, however, that any good to be found under such arrangements of the state exists simply because God in his mercy keeps unbelievers and unbelieving ways of arranging human life from the full consistency that would be as horrible and disastrous as life could be this side of hell.

We have actually never seen the political house liberal democracy builds. Liberal democracy in the post-Enlightenment West has constructed nothing, but has simply squatted in the house Christianity built. Imagine arriving at a person's house and finding it in reasonable shape although it does have some roof tiles off and there is a large hole in one wall. You see a man, 'Liberal Democracy', standing there with bricks in his hands and tools and machines all around him. You are arriving at the arrangement of the state in the United Kingdom in 2007. But you would be badly mistaken if you were to say, 'This is a fine house that "Liberal Democracy" has built for you,' because the fact is that the house was built some generations ago by 'Christian' and what is really happening is that 'Liberal Democracy' is dismantling it as fast as he can, even while claiming the credit for the safety and comfort still to be had in the house. Liberal democracy, as has often been observed, is parasitical and destructive, simultaneously living off the benefits of the influence of the gospel in previous generations *and* working hard to remove them *and* claiming credit for putting them in place.

Objection 15: Put a confessionally Christian state in place and you will end up with horrible intolerance and with punishing people for their beliefs. John Coffey describes how *Lex, rex* is experienced as an 'ambiguous book' by modern readers:

> On the one hand, Rutherford's arguments for popular sovereignty, the rule of law, and the right of resistance to tyranny, remind us of Locke, and can lead to the impression that the author of *Lex, Rex* was something of a modern liberal. On the other hand, his desire for a covenanted nation purged of heresy, idolatry and unbelief, makes him appear thoroughly reactionary, utterly committed to the ideals of Christendom.
>
> (Coffey 1997: 187)

In fact, Rutherford does not suggest for a moment that the state has the right to try to dictate what men and women should or should not believe, far less 'impose' beliefs upon people. In *A Free Disputation against Pretended Liberty of Conscience* (1649) he shows he does believe that it is legitimate for the state to impose negative sanctions upon the public, proveable expression of opinions harmful to others even though those opinions may be conscientiously held (Rutherford 1649: 57–60).

But this 'intolerance' is not exclusive to the confessionally Christian state. If, in our society someone declares publicly and tries to persuade others to believe, for example, that all faithful Muslims will burn eternally in hell; that God hates homosexual sexual activity and everyone who engages in it and does not repent will burn eternally in hell; that people of ethnic group X are of lower intelligence than those of ethnic group Y and are designed by nature to be their servants; or that God created the world in six days something less than 10,000 years ago, then they will experience state-imposed or state-approved negative sanctions ranging from exclusion from public office or from a job with the police through to time in prison.

The question is not, therefore, whether some behaviours, including the public expression of some conscientiously held beliefs, are not legally tolerated. The question is what this intolerance is based on, a matter addressed below.

Objection 16: There are too many detailed questions of biblical exegesis and of public policy to deal with. What would be the punishment for identity theft or for intellectual property theft through the Internet? Would it be legal for Muslims to build a mosque or to preach in the open air? Would everyone be forced to attend church? How would Deuteronomy 13 apply in a state with a Christian constitution? In which activities is a Christian state, as the state, forbidden, allowed and mandated to engage? What if other agencies and institutions fail? How should Christian 'establishment' be recognized? Which churches would be recognized as 'Christian' and who would decide?

These questions are asked as though, unless an answer can be given to them *today*, the entire idea of a confessional Christian state would be undermined. This is a nonsense. There is a vast and beautiful city on a hill and we are climbing towards it. We see the outline of this city and we see that all alternative destinations are ugly and dangerous places. Currently we are hundreds and hundreds of miles away from the city. Should we really curtail our journey just because we are unable to answer questions about the colour of certain doors in the back streets of one quarter, or name the flowers in the window boxes on the other side of the city from us?

A confessionally Christian state will not be established in England for hundreds of years, although we praise God for the possibility that we will see kings as kings bowing down before the Lord Jesus in other countries before then. But although we cannot see the details, the outlines are clear. There is one God, Father, Son and Holy Spirit. His Word, the Bible, is true and authoritative. The Lord Jesus Christ has all authority in heaven and on earth and is the ruler of the kings of the earth. Governments are servants of God, ministers of vengeance, accountable to God to rule according to his will in acknowledgment of the lordship of Jesus. For now, that is enough.

Alternatives to the confessionally Christian state

As mentioned above, all law is imposed morality. All governments, that is, forbid some behaviours on pain of state-imposed negative sanctions. And these behaviours are declared to be 'wrong' (as revealed precisely by the state's imposition of those negative sanctions).

This identification of 'right' and 'wrong' by the state is, however, based upon some ethical authority. The state imposes its morality, and this morality comes from somewhere. The rival ethical authorities are rival bases for law and include force ('might is right'), the will of the majority, intuition, personal preference, tradition, perceived past evolutionary advantage, what 'all decent people' believe and so on.

When the questions 'Why?' and 'How do you know?' and 'But what lies behind *that*?' are pressed, then we will arrive at the ultimate ethical authority for a person or group of persons, including the state. And a person's ultimate ethical authority *is* his god, the incontestible determiner of good and evil, the one beyond whom appeal cannot be made. Rushdoony made these points well:

> Every state is a law order, and every law order represents an enacted
> morality, with procedures for the enforcement of that morality. Every

morality represents a form of theological order, i.e., is an aspect and expression of a religion. The church thus is not the only religious institution; the state also is a religious institution. . . . in any culture the source of law is the god of that society.

(Rushdoony 1986: 7; 1973: 4)

This being the case, in our public theology we may worship (by recognizing as the ultimate ethical authority the imposed morality that is the law) the true God, or a false god, or several gods, or no god. Having given some attention to the confessionally Christian state, that is, a state that has a constitution which explicitly acknowledges the true God as the ultimate ethical authority, we move to consider three possible alternatives to the confessionally Christian state: an explicitly non-Christian confessional state, such as a consistent Muslim would seek; a putatively non-confessional state, such as the humanistic pluralists claim to have; and the mixed and muted confession of 'principled pluralists', which neither denies nor constitutionally acknowledges the universal exclusively ultimate rule of Jesus.

In what follows, then, the 'constitution' is simply a shorthand for 'the declared basis upon which the state is arranged and the criteria by which this or that behaviour is required or forbidden by the state'. The argument below is *not* about the procedures or mechanics of drafting or adopting a Christian constitution in a particular country but is an exercise in public *theology*, examining the theoretical options for the arrangement of the state in regard to its worship of the true God, a false god, no god or several gods.

A false confession: the idolatry of radical Islam
Islam quite openly acknowledges the need for a confessional state. It quite openly declares that all the nations of the world should now, and one day will, have constitutions which contain that confession. It insists that the statute book reflect accurately and consistently what is in the confessional constitution.[6] And Islam then announces

---

6. For modern examples and bibliographical help, see popular analyses of political Islam such as Selbourne 2005; Steyn 2006; Phillips 2006.

an idolatrous confession, one that (1) denies the one true triune God, Father, Son and Holy Spirit, which (2) denies that the Bible is the altogether true, sufficient and authoritative Word of God, and which (3) denies that the Lord Jesus Christ, the Son of God crucified and risen, has been given all authority in heaven and on earth. Islam rebels against the truth of God and replaces it with a lie, and its proposed arrangement of the state is founded upon a false and idolatrous confession. Because Islam is a lie it is also incompetent, sterile and violent, which is heartening, even though the Lord may use it as an instrument of judgment upon the apostate West. And, of course, it remains amusing to watch the secular humanists torn between their multiculturalist approval of Islam on the one hand and their politically correct disapproval of Islam's treatment of women, system of punishment, attitude to homosexual behaviour and disdain for democracy on the other.

No favoured confession: the tyranny of humanistic pluralism
We move to that very humanistic pluralist, a supporter of liberal democracy, proudly claiming that modern society is committed to tolerance and diversity. Such a person will further claim that when it comes to the arrangement of the state, no ideology is privileged. Things are not quite so simple, though, and I have numbered the component parts of the argument in order to make it easier to follow. I have also chosen to use the shorthand 'covenanter' to stand for the proponent of a confessionally Christian state founded upon an explicitly Christian constitution.

1. First, a distinction must be made between the constitution (the ideological or confessional basis for the arrangement of the state that amounts to the identification of the ultimate ethical authority, the groundedness of declaring that certain behaviours are right and certain behaviours are wrong), on the one hand, and the statute book (the list of behaviours legally required and forbidden), on the other hand.
2. Neither the pluralist nor the covenanter believes in an empty statute book: they both believe that certain human behaviours are to be forbidden and, if engaged in should draw down negative sanctions. Murder is an obvious example.

3. Neither the pluralist nor the covenanter believes that the statute book should cover every human action: they both believe there are areas of human behaviour where there should be toleration, that is, if you look up this topic in the statute book you will find nothing: the state will impose no sanctions, negative or positive, in relation to this action. Which football team a person supports, a person's views of his own cleverness or handsomeness, or which colour toothbrush a person uses might fall into this category.

4. So the pluralist and the covenanter both believe in the criminalization of some activities and the toleration of other activities. (And the covenanter believes that there will be many sins – such as pride, untidy bedrooms, impatience and *most* other sinful human behaviours – among the tolerated actions.)

5. What pluralists and covenanters disagree about, then, is *how to determine* which activities should be criminal and which should be tolerated. And the criterion they apply and the authority to which they appeal is, in effect, what they write in their constitution.

6. The *ultimate* constitutional pluralist would write 'everyone is right and no one is right and none of us can ever know for sure' in his constitution. This is a refusal to choose between the gods, to give preference to one ultimate authority claim over others. But it is also a refusal to identify a criterion against which to make decisions as to what is right or wrong, or, more relevantly, to determine what should be in the statute book.

7. This means *either* that the statute book of the ultimate constitutionalist pluralist is empty *or* that those things it contains are there arbitrarily. If there are no grounds whatever upon which decisions as to what should and should not be put in the statute book can be based, then plainly the criminalization of some activities and toleration of others is both arbitrary and unstable.

8. But the arbitrary, unstable and ungrounded criminalization of certain behaviours is tyrannical. The ultimately pluralist state requires and forbids behaviour on no grounds at all: that is tyranny. What starts by looking very tolerant (the refusal to favour any ideology at the constitutional level) ends by being arbitrary and tyrannical. Only a confessional state, one that has

some moral *reason* for criminalizing certain behaviours while tolerating others, avoids tyranny.

9. At this point the constitutional pluralist might retreat somewhat and declare that she *does* have a confession but that it is one that does not decide between competing religious claims. Her constitution (confession) might say, 'We will not take a view upon whether Jesus is Lord and the Bible is sufficient, nor upon Allah and Muhammad, nor upon . . . but we will proceed on the basis of X.' This might be regarded as *intermediate* constitutional pluralism or constitutionalism pluralism *lite*.

10. However, it is not hard to see where this leads. Two questions arise. First, what grounds the decision 'not to take a view upon whether Jesus is Lord'? Second, what is X? It may well be that the answer to each of these two questions is the same: they are, after all, authority questions. Even if the answers to these two questions are not the same initially, sooner or later *either* one will lead to the other as the *ultimate* authority, *or* they will both lead to the identification of another ultimate authority.

11. And *this* ultimate authority, this X, has now become the confessional basis for the arrangement of the state. Possible X's include, 'what all major religions agree on', 'what all decent people think', 'what commands majority support at election time', 'what the expert ethics committees recommend', 'what the random-answer-generator produces each Wednesday lunchtime'.

12. Thus *either* the humanistic pluralist is consistent with his claim not to have a confessional state (to have an empty public square and to be non-ideological), in which case he is arbitrary and tyrannical, *or* he is inconsistent with that claim and proves not to be the pluralist he thought he was. And at that point we are no longer in the business of deciding between 'confession or no confession?' but rather in the business of deciding 'which confession?' The inconsistent humanist pluralist, the intermediate constitutional pluralist has a false confession. The consistent humanist pluralist, the ultimate constitutional pluralist, who initially looks so tolerant, actually proves to be a tyrant.

13. The covenanter, on the other hand, may start the exercise looking terribly intolerant by declaring that his ideological basis

for the arrangement of the state is the fact that 'the Triune God is maker, ruler and judge of all things, the Bible is his infallible and sufficient Word, the Lord Jesus Christ has all authority in heaven and on earth and the civil government is God's servant, an avenger of his wrath on the evil-doer'. However, when *on the basis of the Bible* he then goes on to declare that murder should be criminalized, whereas pride and untidy bedrooms and lust and recreational use of cannabis, though sinful, should not, that is built on a public, wise, righteous and fitting foundation, namely the revealed will of God in the Bible.

14. The apparently generous constitutional pluralist is a tyrant and the toleration he offers is arbitrary and unstable; the apparently narrow covenanter actually requires, forbids and tolerates behaviours on a firm and righteous basis: the revealed will of the triune Creator.

15. Humanistic constitutional pluralism is unstable: either it opts for an ideological basis (it goes intermediate and confesses its 'god') and so ceases to be constitutional pluralism, or it refuses to confess its 'god', in which case it makes whoever manages to have power at the moment the god: an inscrutable, unaccountable, arbitrary and thus tyrannical god.

Even in this mess, there is much reason to give thanks to God. In his mercy he keeps back the unregenerate from consistency with their presuppositions, and a large part of humanist inconsistency is its use of stolen Christian goods. Admittedly as we saw above, this is confusing because it can give the false impression, in the short term of three or four generations, that humanist pluralism can actually work! This God-granted inconsistency of the humanists is also a mercy to others because it means that life is not as bad as it might be even in a gospel-rejecting country. And there is further encouragement in the thought that the more consistent humanists become, the less effectively they will function in God's world.[7]

---

7. The argument advanced above is best related to Rutherford's own work through what he says about the formal cause of government in chapters XXII to XXVII. Rutherford argues that what makes government *government*

A mixed and muted confession: the confusion of Christian 'principled pluralism'

It is not an easy matter to define Christian 'principled pluralism', but there are three things it might mean.

First, Christian 'principled pluralism' might mean the proposal that a state has a Christian confession combined with wide definitions of 'toleration'. Such a proposal may arise out of a misplaced fear that espousal of full-blooded Christian confessionalism involves commitment to a particularly small number of tolerated behaviours or to the enforcement of personal Christian confession or suchlike. This, however, is not a distinct position, but simply a variant of Christian confessionalism because it assumes that explicit acknowledgment of the triune God, the lordship of Jesus and the authority of Scripture form the proper constitutional foundation for the state. It differs from other Christian confessionalisms not at the level of the 'constitution' (identification of the ultimate ethical authority) but at the level of the 'statute book' (making specific moves, on the basis of the ultimate ethical authority, to criminalizing some behaviours and tolerating others). This version of 'principled pluralism' actually desires a confessionally Christian state and simply needs to hold discussions with others who have the same desire about what Scripture, rightly read, teaches should be on the 'statute book'. It argues not that there is more than one ultimate ethical authority, but rather that that ultimate ethical authority (the God who speaks in Scripture) requires wider 'statute book' toleration than it fears other Christian confessionalisms allow.

Second, and just conceivably, some Christian 'principled pluralists' might occupy the same ground (in respect of the public square) as ultimate constitutional pluralists, claiming that we should have an 'empty public square', that is, no recognition of an ultimate ethical authority for the actions of the state. These Christians

---

Footnote 7 (*cont.*)

    is its submissive and subordinate embodiment of the law of God. His argument is developed in terms of the 'law' and the 'king' along similar lines to those of the argument above, where reference has been to the 'confession/constitution' and the 'statute book'.

would gladly affirm that the triune God is the true God, that Jesus is Lord, and that the Bible is authoritative, but they would claim that a proper reading of the Bible teaches that these things should not be authoritatively (constitutionally) affirmed in the public square. They believe that although the triune God is the true God, that Jesus is Lord, and that the Bible is authoritative, God does not want nations as political entities and governments as law-making bodies to acknowledge this. However, this is not a distinct position: it is the same as humanistic pluralism and subject to the same criticisms (see above).

Third, some Christian 'principled pluralists' might recognize the need for a confession (the state's explicit identification of the ethical authority for its actions) but deny that such a confession should be explicitly or exclusively Christian. At the level of the confession, favour should not be extended to one particular god. It asserts that there could be multiple, contradictory but legitimate, theologically grounded ideological *bases* for identifying right and wrong. That is, no decision will be made between Islam, Judaism, atheism and Christianity, for example, but nevertheless, murder will be forbidden.

The weakness of this position has already been exposed above. This position calls itself 'pluralist' because it allows a number of distinct confessions together to form the basis of the state. In reality, however, this amounts to the identification of a common denominator confession (see above).

For a number of reasons it is a dismal thing when Christians adopt this position. First, the 'pluralist' confession of such a view in effect asserts that there is a part of life in which we are not to affirm that Jesus is Lord and/or that there is a part of life in which we can operate well (effectively and faithfully) while not taking a view upon whether or not Jesus is Lord. This means that operationally and ideologically this sphere (the sphere in which the 'we should not or do not need to confess that Jesus is Lord' confession holds) is idolatrous and/or polytheistic because in this sphere Jesus is lord along with other lords.

It also means that there are whole areas of activity and thought (wherever the various acknowledged lords disagree) on which no judgment is given. That is, there may be something King Jesus declares to be a crime but the state is not to declare to be a crime, because Baal or Isis or Allah disagree with Jesus. False gods have a veto on the wishes of the true God.

And if the state continues to give no judgment in these areas, then it *has* actually moved to a confession. If it gives a judgment in an area of life over which the various acknowledged lords disagree, then it *either* sides against Jesus, in which case it has left X and adopted a false confession, *or* it sides with Jesus, in which case it has left X and adopted a Christian confession.

This will not do. The X that Christian 'principled pluralists' (Christian versions of the *intermediate* constitutional pluralists above) attempt to confess is not (by definition) an explicit recognition of the exclusive and universal lordship of Jesus, and is therefore a false confession. It is unstable and must resolve either into the tyranny of no confession, the idolatry of false confession, or the no-longer-pluralism of true Christian confession. X conflicts with the biblical data that all nations and rulers are subject to Christ and must acknowledge that (Pss 2, 72; Dan. 2, 4; Matt. 28; Rom. 13; Phil. 2; Col. 1; Rev. 1).

And when we ask what precisely X is and where it comes from, the answer usually resolves into some version of natural law. This might be framed in terms of 'the common ground between the world's major religions' or in terms of 'what all right-thinking people agree upon', but natural law is what it is. The problem with this, of course, is that a 'natural law' which conflicts with the Bible comes from our sinful hearts, not from the general revelation of the God who speaks consistently; and a 'natural law' which tells us that there are parts of life over which Jesus is not to be confessed as Lord nor the Bible acknowledged as his Word, parts of life in which we can function in a way pleasing to God without Jesus-Bible acknowledgment and dependence is satanic.

There are three versions of the natural law argument we should take into account.[8] One version is founded upon the separation of the realm of nature and the realm of grace and asserts that since

---

8. See Daniel Strange's chapter in this book for a more thorough analysis and for bibliographical leads.

nature has not been as badly damaged by sin as others think, then the unregenerate can function effectively in the nature 'compartment' in certain matters and we can talk to them using 'nature' language and arguments.

A second version is founded upon the separation of the law and the gospel and asserts that there are two 'kingdoms', one associated with the law and one with the gospel. Although we want everyone personally to move from law to gospel and thus into the kingdom of light, yet a part of human life is always to be a 'law' part: the civil, extra-ecclesial part of life. The gospel makes no difference to the operation of that part of life because it is a separate 'kingdom' as ordered by God.

The third version of the natural law argument is founded upon the separation of creation and redemption as historical realms of God's involvement with humankind. Even though the fall has spoiled things, yet there is creation or common grace that is a discernible residue of creation realities according to which people can still think, communicate and function. Redemption restores creation, but before and apart from redemption there is creation grace, and even after and with redemption for an individual there are still parts of human existence unaddressed by redemption revelation and thus to be lived by creation grace.

What these three have in common is that the world or human existence is divided into spheres or realms, that it is possible for the unregenerate to function in the lower- or prior-realm in some matters, and inevitable that some parts of life will continue to be ordered by lower- or prior-realm principles, even for the regenerate. Being human is all that is required to get by reasonably in these parts of life.

This means that, according to these theories, we can address issues in a nature/law/creation sort of way without needing (theologically or rhetorically) to talk about Jesus or the Bible.

Over against all this stands full-blooded Christian confessionalism, what might be called theocratic, whole-Bible presuppositionalism, which asserts that there is no division in human life because every piece of territory and aspect of life is owned by and under the authority of the Lord Jesus Christ, and every human activity is definitely and sufficiently addressed by the Bible. There are not 'non-Jesus' or 'non-Bible' parts of human existence. There are unregenerate people, but they manage to survive, communicate, function in some sense as human beings *not* because they live in a distinct ('merely' nature/law/creation) sphere but because, rebels though they are, they live with the overspill of Jesus-Bible rule or by stealing Jesus-Bible things or by adopting Jesus-Bible ways. When they do this, they are being inconsistent with their true (Jesus-Bible-hating) selves and yet this is the only way they function at all as humans.

That is, the true government over *everything* is Jesus-Bible government. The Jesus-Bible government provides air and water for all in its territory. There are quite a few people who hold out against the rightful authority of this Jesus-Bible government and yet they do so while using Jesus-Bible air and water. They function as human beings not by living in a different territory or under a different government but precisely because of Jesus-Bible rule.

For the loyal subjects of the Jesus-Bible realm to try to help the rebels but not mention Jesus or the Bible is a dishonour to the rightful King and no help at all to these rebels because it reinforces their sense that they have found a little corner where Jesus-Bible does not rule and yet where they seem to get along fine.

There is one world and there is one government. Some people live according to that. Others refuse to recognize it and live as though there were other governments (ways of being human) than the Jesus-Bible way. They get away with this because operationally in some matters they live the Jesus-Bible way, even while declaring that they do not. It helps them not at all to teach them the falsehood that actually there are two legitimate governments and that while (some aspects of) life can be better under Jesus-Bible government, nevertheless the other (nature/law/creation) government does have legitimacy.

This being the case, it is worth asking why some Christians persist in their appeal to X (whether labelled 'natural law' or 'common-denominator confessionalism' or 'what the major world religions have in common' or something else). If the answers have to do with gaining a hearing or broadening the appeal of the Christian contribution to political debate, then the question arises whether in gaining the hearing the 'principled pluralist' has muted the message. If to gain a hearing for the gospel we have to agree not to mention Jesus' name then it is not the gospel that will be heard. If the reason for appealing to X and asserting that no exclusive confession should form the constitution is a short-term tactical move (like Christians claiming tax relief or freedom of religion), then we must not forget that such a political ceasefire holds only until 'one side is ready to resume the fight to the death'.

Summary and conclusion

In summary, I have stated in this chapter that Samuel Rutherford's view of government amounts to a demand for a confessionally Christian state, a covenanted nation. I have explored a little of what that means, responded to the most common objections to it, and evaluated the three current alternatives to a confessionally Christian state. The first alternative, that of Islam and other false religions, is a false confession and is idolatrous. The second alternative, that of humanistic pluralism, is no-confession and is tyrannical. The third alternative, that of Christian 'principled pluralism', is of multiple confessions and is confused and unstable, either giving unbelief a veto or resolving into the tyranny or idolatry of the other positions, or, blessedly, abandoning 'pluralism' and joining Christian confessionalism.

To those who respond that this is not a 'gospel' matter and that it should be no concern of ours, the reply is simple. Graeme Goldsworthy reminds us that 'the gospel is the proclamation of what God has done in Christ, and needs always to be distinguished from the fruit of the gospel, which is God's work in those who believe'.[9] It is clear, even from mere lexical studies,[10] that 'what God

---

9. Goldsworthy 2000: 523.

10. See the general usage of the 'evangel' words in the Septuagint associated with the death of the old and the accession of the new king and with the beginning of new rule in 1 Sam. 31:9; 2 Sam. 1:20; 4:10; 18:19, 20, 22, 25, 26, 27, 31; 1 Kgs 1:42; 2 Kgs 7:9; 1 Chr. 10:9; Pss 40:9; 68:11; 96:2; Jer. 20:15; Nah. 1:15. See also how in Isaiah God arrives, redeems, reigns, how

has done in Christ' (and is therefore announced in the gospel) is
bring about the end of the old regime and establish the new, accom-
plishing dynastic transfer so that rule has passed to the rightful Lord,
whose empire will dwarf all previous empires and whose kingdom
will have no end. Once we understand the inescapably 'political'
dimension to the gospel summed up in the words 'Jesus is Lord',
then we see that what humanism, false religions and inconsistent
Christian confessions do is deny or dilute the gospel. And we will
further see that a proper part of gospel commitment is our recognition and desire that the state should be confessionally Christian.

The words of the Lord Jesus Christ may be applied to societies
as well as to individuals:

> Everyone then who hears these words of mine and does them will be
> like a wise man who built his house on the rock. And the rain fell, and
> the floods came, and the winds blew and beat on that house, but it did
> not fall, because it had been founded on the rock. And everyone who
> hears these words of mine and does not do them will be like a foolish
> man who built his house on the sand. And the rain fell, and the floods
> came, and the winds blew and beat against that house, and it fell, and
> great was the fall of it.
>
> (Matt. 7:24–27)

If a nation builds its house on the sand of a false confession, then
it will be destroyed. If a nation attempts to build its house in the
air of no confession, then the house will come down to earth: on
to rock or sand. If a nation attempts to build half on the sand and
half on the rock or on the mud in between ('principled pluralism'),
then it cannot stay there but must decide on the foundation it
really seeks, and its destiny will follow from that. But the obvious

---

Footnote 10 (*cont.*)

he rules to save etc.: Isa. 40:9; 52:7; 60:6; 61:1. Compare this with use of
the 'evangel' words in first-century Rome: good news of a global Lord,
divine Son and cosmic Saviour, and the reflection of this in important
New Testament texts: Mark 1:1, 14–15; Rom. 1:1, 15–17. For more detail,
see http://www.davidpfield.com/other/Evangel+.pdf.

application of Matthew 7:24–27 to the political foundation of
societies is, 'Build your house, that is, arrange your state on the
rock of Jesus and his words.' Samuel Rutherford and the consistently Reformed tradition of political thought that has followed
him have, by arguing for and seeking the covenanted nation of a
confessionally Christian state, helped us understand better what it
will mean to do just that.

Further reading

Chaplin, J. (2005), 'Political Theology', in K. Vanhoozer et al. (eds.), *Dictionary for Theological Interpretation of the Bible* (Grand Rapids: Baker), 597–600.

DeMar, G. (2004), *Myths, Lies, and Half-Truths* (Powder Springs: American Vision).

Eliot, T. S. (1939), *The Idea of a Christian Society* (London: Faber & Faber).

Field, D. (2007), 'Not the Least Lash Lost' http://davidpfield.com/other/AAPC2-3lecture.pdf (accessed 8 Sept. 2007).

The Form and Order of Service . . . Observed in The Coronation of Her Majesty Queen Elizabeth II . . . 1953 (2007) http://www.oremus.org/liturgy/coronation/index.html (accessed 8 Sept. 2007).

Garver, S. J. (2007), 'There Is Another King: Gospel as Politics' http://www.joelgarver.com/writ/phil/politics.htm (accessed 8 Sept. 2007).

Hoppe, H. (2001), *Democracy, The God that Failed* (London: Transaction).

The Instrument of Government, 1654 (2007) http://www.olivercromwell.org/protectorate/protectorate_6.htm (accessed 8 Sept. 2007).

Leithart, P. J. (2003), *Against Christianity* (Moscow: Canon).

Mackay, D. (2005), 'The Crown Rights of King Jesus Today', in Clark (2005: 210–259).

The National Covenant of 1638 (2007), http://www.constitution.org/eng/conpur023.htm (accessed 8 Sept. 2007).

North, G. (1989), *Political Polytheism: The Myth of Pluralism* (Tyler: Institute for Christian Economics).

O'Donovan, O. (2005), *The Ways of Judgment* (Grand Rapids: Eerdmans).

Olliff, D. (2007), 'The Return of the King' http://www.davidpfield.com/other/Olliff-Gospel-King.pdf (accessed 8 Sept. 2007).

Perks, S. (1998), *In Defence of the Christian State* (Taunton: Kuyper Foundation).

Schlossberg, H. (1983), *Idols for Destruction* (Wheaton: Crossway).

The Solemn League and Covenant of 1643 (2007), http://www.constitution.org/eng/conpuro58.htm (accessed 8 Sept. 2007).

Wilson, D., and Jones, D. (1998), *Angels in the Architecture* (Moscow: Canon).

Wright, N. T. (2005), *Fresh Perspective* (London: SPCK).

— (2007a), 'God and Caesar, Then and Now' http://www.ntwrightpage.com/Wright_God_Caesar.pdf (accessed 8 Sept. 2007).

— (2007b), 'Paul's Gospel and Caesar's Empire' http://www.ctinquiry.org/publications/wright.htm (accessed 8 Sept. 2007).

4. GABBATHA AND GOLGOTHA: PENAL SUBSTITUTIONARY ATONEMENT AND THE PUBLIC SQUARE

Garry J. Williams

> Oh, East is East, and West is West, and never the twain shall meet.
>> (Rudyard Kipling, 'The Ballad of East and West')

Introduction: the cross and politics

The cross and politics: East and West?
The cross and politics may seem like an impossible or even dangerous combination, in which the former will surely lose out to the latter, the gospel to merely worldly concerns. There are abundant cautionary tales of the death and resurrection of the Lord Jesus being reduced to an example of the victory of the politically weak over the politically powerful, set forth in the service of a theology that amounts to little more than baptized Marxism.

This is where many who identify themselves as classical evangelicals fear that public theology will take them. They suspect that public theology is a Trojan horse, a subtle way for culture to assume control of theology. If this were so, then it must indeed be avoided, since the domination of theology by culture makes theology a mere mirror – indeed a rather clouded and useless mirror – of culture. This is the point of Tyrrell's famous picture of liberal theology: the liberal looks for Jesus, but 'looking back through nineteen centuries of Catholic darkness' he finds 'only the reflection of a Liberal Protestant face, seen at the bottom of a deep well'.[1] Thus liberalism is narcissistic, and in attempting to understand God by studying humanity it is, as J. Gresham Machen argued, 'pantheizing' (Machen 1923: 63). If thinking about the relationship between the cross and politics really does mean dragging this kind of thing in through the gates, then we must totally avoid it. But does it necessarily entail this? Might we safely consider together the doctrine of the cross and issues of public theology? More specifically, can we safely employ key political concepts such as law, authority and judgment in formulating the doctrine of the cross?[2]

The connection in Reformed writings

The Reformed tradition provides extensive material that encourages us to do exactly this. In a range of sixteenth-century texts, especially those written for catechetical purposes, the political realities that surrounded the Lord Jesus in his trial and crucifixion are repeatedly deployed in the construction of the doctrine of the atonement. Here for example, is a series of questions and answers from the 1545 edition of John Calvin's catechism, written for use with the children of Geneva. This particular exchange appears during the discussion of the statement in the Apostles' Creed that Christ 'suffered under Pontius Pilate':

> *Minister:* Why do you not say simply in one word that he died instead of adding also the name of the governor under whom he suffered?
> *Child:* This has reference not only to our credence of the story, but that we may know his death to be connected with his condemnation.
> *M:* Explain this more clearly.

---

1. The image is a summary of Alfred Loisy's criticism of Adolf von Harnack; see Tyrrell 1910: 44.
2. For an exploration of the definition of key political concepts derived from Scripture, see O'Donovan 1996.

C: He died so that the penalty owed by us might be discharged, and he
might exempt us from it. But since we all, because we are sinners, were
offensive to the judgment of God, in order to stand in our stead, he
desired to be arraigned before an earthly judge, and to be condemned by
his mouth, so that we might be acquitted before the heavenly tribunal of
God.

M: But Pilate pronounces him innocent (Matt. 27:23; Luke 23:14), and
hence does not condemn him as a malefactor.

C: Both things must be considered. For the judge bears testimony to his
innocence, so that there may be evidence that he suffered not for his
own misdeeds but for ours. Nevertheless at the same time he is formally
condemned by the same judge to make it plain that he suffered as our
surety the judgment which we deserved, that thus he might free us from
guilt.

M: Well said. For if he were a sinner, he would not be a fit surety to pay
the penalty of another's sin. Nevertheless, that his condemnation might
secure our acquittal, it was requisite that he be reckoned among the
malefactors (Isa. 53:12).

C: So I understand it.

(Calvin 1954: 98)

The same pattern is also present in later editions of the *Institutes
of the Christian Religion*, where Calvin makes the same point about
the innocence and condemnation of Jesus and then goes on
to elaborate at greater length the significance of his death by
crucifixion:

> To take away our condemnation, it was not enough for him to suffer any
> kind of death: to make satisfaction for our redemption a form of death
> had to be chosen in which he might free us both by transferring our
> condemnation to himself and by taking our guilt upon himself. If he had
> been murdered by thieves or slain in an insurrection by a raging mob, in
> such a death there would have been no evidence of satisfaction. But
> when he was arraigned before the judgment seat as a criminal, accused
> and pressed by testimony, and condemned by the mouth of the judge to
> die – we know by these proofs (*his documentis*) that he took the role of a
> guilty man and evildoer.

(Calvin 1960, 1: 509 [2.16.5])

The material that we have here invites further investigation. On the one hand, it might be taken to imply simply that Pilate's involvement in Jesus' death reveals the cross to be a kind of condemnation before a judge. On this reading, Pilate plays a merely revelatory role: he is present in the story simply to alert us to the fact that Jesus is being condemned for our sins. On the other hand, Pilate might function not just as a sign to alert us to God's legal sentence upon Christ, but also as the very instrument by which that legal sentence is imposed. On this instrumental reading, Jesus is judged by God by being judged by Pilate. In other words, the abandonment of Jesus to the cross is part of the way in which the Father hands the Son over to the punishment for our sins.

The child's first answer in the *Catechism* passage establishes the revelatory reading: 'that we may know his death to be connected with his condemnation'. In the second answer, however, Pilate's role is clearly also instrumental: 'in order to stand in our stead (*quo vicem nostrum subiret*), he desired to be arraigned before an earthly judge' (the Latin is from Calvin 1667: 14). Both elements are likewise present in the extract from the *Institutes*. The judgment by Pilate serves as a proof (*documentum*) for us that he took the place of sinners, and the death had to be by crucifixion to be what it was, satisfaction.

The instrumental meaning is similarly suggested by the use of the word 'thereby' in the Heidelberg Catechism (1563):

> Question 38: *Why did He suffer 'under Pontius Pilate' as his judge?*
> Answer 38: *That he, being innocent, might be condemned by an earthly judge, and thereby set us free from the judgment of God which, in all its severity, ought to fall upon us.*
>
> (Noll 1991: 144)

The precise sense of the instrumentality is explained more clearly by one of the authors of the catechism, Caspar Olevianus, in his commentary:

> One must look to God as the one who pronounced the judgment through the mouth of Pilate, for judgment is of God (2 Chr. 19:6). When Christ was put on trial here on earth as an evildoer, He was being

tried before God, laden with your sin and my sin and that of the whole
world, so that He might take the judgment of our damnation and
punishment upon himself. We should have been brought before the
judgment seat of God and received the sentence of damnation, but
Christ took our damnation upon Himself. For that reason He had to be
brought to trial as if He were each of us, and He had to be sentenced
and condemned to death by God Himself through Pilate the judge, who
of course had something quite different in mind.

(Olevianus 1995: 65)

Olevianus thus explains further the instrumental role of Pilate's
judgment. He posits double agency in the trial of Jesus: Pilate's
words were at one and the same time the sentence of Pilate and
the sentence of God. Pilate's sentence is in some senses identified
with God's, yet they remain distinct.

In this tradition of Reformed commentary on the Apostles'
Creed, the penal doctrine of the atonement is woven from the
fabric of reflection on Jesus' encounter with human political
authorities. Not only is political language used, but the very nature
of the atonement is constituted and revealed through political
events. Thus the historical circumstances of Jesus' death establish
a connection between the cross and politics. If we are to take seriously the fact that God reveals himself in history, and if we are to
avoid abstracting the doctrine of the atonement from the history
of Jesus, Israel and the world, then our doctrine of the atonement
must be rooted here.

Some modern writers have failed to recognize the significance
accorded to the historical circumstances of Jesus' death for the
Reformed doctrine of the atonement. For example, J. Denny
Weaver argues that 'the various versions of satisfaction atonement
concern a legal construct or an abstract formula that functions
outside of and apart from history', and that 'the legal paradigm of
the satisfaction atonement images is ahistorical' (Weaver 2001: 69,
80). These Reformed texts expose such criticisms as mere carica-
tures of the historic doctrine; Calvin and Olevianus clearly grasped
that they needed to construct the penal doctrine from the details
of the trial of Jesus. They are unequivocal: it must be this death in
this political context.

The connection in John's Gospel

The connection between political concepts and the cross is also
elucidated by other details of the Gospels, such as the way John
describes the trial before Pilate. John's account is replete with the
language and concepts of politics.

The arrest

The context of the trial narrative raises the question of authority.
Following the Farewell Discourse and the prayer of John 17, the
trial narrative is preceded by John's account of the arrest of Jesus.
When approached by his captors, Jesus identifies himself by using
the unpredicated divine name 'I am' (*egō eimi*), and the arresting
party falls to the ground before him (18:5–6). John intends us to
see here a disclosure of Jesus' divine authority. We thus find the
account of the trial of Jesus introduced by an episode that gives us
an astonishing glimpse of his full authority over his enemies, and
therefore over the events that are about to befall him. It is then no
surprise when Jesus secures the release of his followers, when he
voluntarily orders Peter to sheathe his sword, or when we repeatedly read that the events occur to fulfil Scripture or the words of
Jesus himself.

Justice

From within the two trial narratives themselves, we note three
political themes: justice, authority and judgment. In the trial before
Annas (18:19–24), we find a concern for the processes of justice.
Jesus affirms the public character of his ministry, and asks his
opponents similarly to bear public witness to his supposed wrongdoing. This is a particularly poignant request given the emphasis
earlier in the Gospel on the role of witnesses. In chapter 5, for
example, Jesus is concerned to demonstrate that he is not his own
only witness. Rather John the Baptist bore witness to him, as do
the Father and the Scriptures, especially Moses (5:31–47). Later, in
chapter 8, Jesus is prepared to say that he bears witness to himself,
but he continues to emphasize the witness of the Father. Together,
he and the Father provide the two witnesses required in the law to
which he himself refers (Deut. 19:15; John 8:17). By chapter 18, at
the point of the trial, we know full well that witnesses matter, an

impression confirmed when Jesus describes to Pilate his own role
as a witness to the truth (18:37).

Authority
Second, the issue of legal authority looms large in the seven scenes
of the trial before Pilate. The Jews involve Pilate in Jesus' trial
because although they have a law by which they think Jesus must
die (19:7), they do not have the authority to implement it (*ouk
exestin*, 18:31). When Pilate asks Jesus whether he is a king and
what he has done (scene 2), Jesus grants that he is indeed a king,
but explains that his kingship is not from this world (*ek tou kosmou
toutou*). Then in scene 6 (which corresponds to scene 2 in the chiastic arrangement highlighted by Stibbe), Pilate threatens Jesus by
pointing out that he has the authority to release him or to crucify
him, and Jesus replies by telling Pilate that he would have no
authority (*exousia*) unless it were given him from above.[3] This
amounts to a claim that he himself is the source of Pilate's authority, since Jesus is the one who comes 'from above' (*egō ek tōn anō
eimi*, 8:23).

The question of authority is focused in the depiction of Jesus as
the true king in the ironic royal epiphany of chapter 19. Jesus is
proclaimed king by Pilate, he is invested with the emblems of
royalty, he is received by the soldiers as king, and subsequently he
is enthroned, lifted up, on the cross (the references can be traced
from Stibbe 1993: 191). Stibbe explains how the irony functions:
'the narrator sets up a distinction between what characters within
the narrative world can see, and what the paradigmatic reader

---

3. The chiastic arrangement of seven scenes is described in Stibbe 1993:
187:

A[1] 18:28–32   Outside: the Jews demand Jesus' death.
B[1] 18:33–38a Inside: Pilate questions Jesus about kingship.
C[1] 18:38b–40 Outside: Pilate finds Jesus innocent. Barabbas is chosen.
D   19:1–3   Inside: the soldiers humiliate Jesus.
C[2] 19:4–8   Outside: Pilate finds Jesus innocent. 'Behold the man!'
B[2] 19:9–11   Inside: Pilate talks with Jesus about authority.
A[2] 19:12–16a Outside: the Jews secure the death sentence.

standing above this world can see' (197). In the royal epiphany the characters see only mockery, whereas the readers see the truth that Jesus is the one with kingly authority.

Judgment
The third theme, judgment, is closely connected to the issue of authority, since the one who rules also judges.[4] John repeatedly deploys his favoured device of irony to show that Jesus, not Pilate, is the king and judge. Andrew Lincoln explains: 'the accused becomes the accuser, the one on trial becomes the judge, and from the first words of Jesus, Pilate is put on the defensive, put on trial' (Lincoln 2000: 126). The theme of judgment reaches its high point when Pilate sits down on 'the judgment seat at a place called The Pavement, and in Hebrew, Gabbatha' (19:13). Now is the moment when Pilate will sit down to pronounce sentence on Jesus. Or is it? The Greek text at this point is noted for its ambiguity: an alternative translation is possible in which Pilate places Jesus on the seat of judgment. The verb used here (*kathizō*) can be intransitive (implying that Pilate himself sat down), or transitive (implying that he seated Jesus). It is clear from Matthew 27:19 that at some point Pilate himself sat down to pronounce judgment, but this does not preclude the possibility that Jesus was also seated. Many commentators think that the ambiguity at this point is deliberate, one of the ways in which John emphasizes the two levels at which his story can be read.[5] Even if John definitely intended to depict Jesus

---

4. For an argument for the identity of Jesus as King and Judge based on the connection of the two concepts in Isaiah, e.g. 11:1–10 and 41:21, see Lincoln 2000: 135.

5. Lincoln objects to the idea of deliberate ambiguity because at no other points does John rely on an ambiguity of grammar to state his irony (Lincoln 2000: 134). But this is hardly prohibitive; who are we to say that John cannot do something only once? Lincoln also argues that it cannot be Pilate who sits, because he has not been depicted as sitting on the seat before, and because he never pronounces a formal verdict on Jesus. Neither of these arguments is persuasive since they both apply equally to Matthew, where Pilate is clearly the one seated: he appears thus in 27:19

as being seated, as for example Justin Martyr would later, the irony of the position of Jesus as judge would remain (Justin Martyr 1995, 1: 174 [35]). This is all the more striking when we remember that the term for the judgment seat (*bēma*) is used in Scripture of both earthly (Acts 12:21; 25:6) and divine thrones (Rom. 14:10), and even of the judgment seat of Christ (2 Cor. 5:10).

Thus John constructs his proclamation of the kingship and judgment of Jesus by deploying and ironically inverting the political figures and concepts in his narrative. In this way he shows that Jesus is the true king who judges, and he emphasizes the wonder that the judge is now judged instead of his people, echoing the irony of Caiaphas' statement in John 11:50. In the light of such evidence, the close relationship between the doctrine of the atonement and political concepts is indisputable. This does not establish the precise nature or content of the relationship, but if we find the combination of the cross and politics alarming, then we have a problem with John.

> Oh, East is East, and West is West, and never the twain shall meet
> Till Earth and Sky stand presently at God's great Judgment Seat.

The cross and politics may seem like East and West, but according to John they have already met at the 'great Judgment Seat' of Gabbatha.

Outline

Having established that we must integrate the doctrine of the atonement with political concepts, we now consider the path ahead.[6] I will address the relationship between penal substitutionary atonement and public theology from two sides, looking at the

---

with no prior mention of the seat, and never pronounces a formal verdict on Jesus (Lincoln thinks that v. 24 is a verdict, but it is simply an act of self-exculpation).

6. This is an appropriate point for me to note my gratitude to Steve Jeffery and Tom Watts for their technical assistance in preparing this chapter for publication.

influence of the public square on theology, and of theology on the public square. In Part 1, we will explore the place of political concepts in forming the doctrine of the atonement by examining the so-called Governmental Theory – a signal attempt to read the atonement politically by Hugo Grotius, the seventeenth-century Dutch jurist and politician. Grotius' position is commonly regarded as an overtly political revision of penal substitutionary atonement, and therefore allows us to address whether a sustained attempt to illuminate the atonement with political concepts is helpful or misleading.

In Part 2, we will examine the influence of penal substitutionary atonement on the public square. I will take a thoroughly theological approach to this issue, starting with considerations that lie a long way back from the daily questions of political action. By reflecting theologically on the political actions surrounding the death of Jesus, I will lay foundations for the construction of political ethics. Here I follow the example of Oliver O'Donovan in his work *The Desire of the Nations*: 'Political theology – as a *theoretic* discipline, though not detached from experience and engagement – must precede political ethics' (O'Donovan 1996: 15). My task, though, is much more modest. Where O'Donovan seeks to establish the basic concepts of political theology itself, I will simply explore the atonement in order to understand a little more of the connection between divine and human rule. The questions are therefore specific. Does penal substitutionary atonement entail a conception of God and his justice that is ethically useless? Still worse, do we find a doctrine that has negative ethical consequences, for example in the realms of politics and justice? Or does penal substitution itself contain resources to prevent rulers using it to justify immoral political acts? Indeed might the doctrine even provide foundations for understanding the limits and boundaries of political authority?

Part 1: from the public square to the cross

Critics of Grotius' doctrine of the atonement have claimed that his Governmental Theory owes more to his seventeenth-century political ideals than it does to Scripture. R. W. Dale, for example, comments that for Grotius 'the Divine administration of the universe was but a higher form of that political life with which he was so well acquainted' (Dale 1899: 294). Perhaps the very name of the theory has reinforced that impression, but as Justin Martyr protested to the emperor Antoninus Pius, 'by the mere application of a name, nothing is decided' (Justin Martyr 1995, 1: 163 [4]). We must, therefore, look beyond the title of the 'Governmental Theory' to see whether Grotius does indeed allow the public square instead of special revelation to dictate his theology of the atonement.

In my judgment, Grotius did not hold many of the views regularly attributed to him.[7] Here, however, we must narrow our attention to two claims he certainly did make. The first is that in the atonement God acts as the ruler (*Rector*) of the universe; the second is that God acts in the atonement to demonstrate his justice.

Grotius on God as ruler

Grotius emphasizes that in the doctrine of the atonement God should be thought of as the ruler of the universe. He agrees with Socinus in rejecting the simple conception of God as judge in the atonement. A judge, he argues, is under the law by virtue of his office, so if God were merely a judge, he would not be free to do anything other than punish sinners:

> Such a judge could not liberate a guilty person from punishment, not even by transferring the punishment to someone else, not because this would in itself be unjust, but because it would be incongruous with the law which he himself has been chosen to serve.
>
> (Grotius 1990: 133 [2.3])

---

7. I hope to provide a critique of the standard interpretation of Grotius on another occasion. In short, I would argue that the text of *De satisfactione* does not claim that God should be thought of as a ruler *rather than* a judge in the atonement; it does not describe the justice demonstrated in the cross as simply an expedient of government that bears no relation to the divine being, and it does not teach that the cross saves solely by being a deterrent from sin.

Despite this agreement with Socinus, Grotius rejects the heretic's view that God should be conceived as simply an offended party. This, Grotius thinks, 'may almost be said to be in this matter his fundamental mistake' (135 [2.4]). For Grotius, it is only as ruler and not as judge or an offended party that God has the authority not to punish sinners. Only the author of the law may sanction deliverance from its just sentence:

> To inflict punishment, or to liberate from punishment someone whom
> you can punish – which Scripture calls 'justify' – , is the exclusive
> prerogative of the ruler as such, as it is of the father in a family, of the
> king in a state, and of God in the universe.
>
>   (133 [2.1])

A ruler may relax the strict sentence of the law because in his realm he (or one previously in his office) is the one who gave it in the first place. Certainly then, Grotius thinks of God as the ruler of creation in his doctrine of the atonement.

Grotius on the demonstration of divine justice

Grotius teaches that God acts to demonstrate his justice in the atonement. This emerges in his description of the twofold end of the cross: 'the demonstration of divine justice, and the remission of sins with respect to us, i.e. our impunity' (117 [1.40]). He proceeds to explain the first by expounding Paul's argument in Romans 3:25–26:

> Here, in close connection with 'blood', i.e. the bloody death, stands the
> end, 'to demonstrate his *dikaiosyne* ("justice")'. By the expression 'justice'
> of God is not to be understood that justice which God brings about in
> us or which he imputes to us, but that which is in God; for he continues:
> 'that he himself might be just', i.e. appear to be just.[8]
>
>   (117 [1.41])

It is thus clear that Grotius regards God as the ruler of the universe, and that he views the atonement as a demonstration of

---

8. I have corrected the punctuation of this quotation.

divine justice. But where does he find these ideas? Is he simply engaging in natural theology, envisaging God as merely an over-sized civil magistrate? Is the Pensionary of Rotterdam staring down the well and seeing just an exaggerated reflection of his own face? It is to this question that we now turn.

God as ruler

Many biblical books maintain that God is the ruler of the world on the grounds that he is its creator. For example, Psalm 24 declares:

> The earth is the LORD's and the fullness thereof,
>   the world and those who dwell therein;
> for (*kî*) he has founded it upon the seas,
>   and established it upon the rivers.
> (vv. 1–2)

The creation narrative itself, by depicting him delegating rule (*rādâ*) to humankind (Gen. 1:26), assumes that God rules the creation. It also reveals the Lord as the lawgiver, and as the one who curses the breach of the law (2:17; 3:14–19).

This combination of God exercising his rule and giving laws is seen most clearly in his dealings with Israel. Most obviously, he gave the Law at Sinai, but the divine rule over redeemed Israel began with the exodus itself, for the rejection of Yahweh's kingship implicit in Israel's demand for a human king is said to have been continuous 'from the day I brought them up out of Egypt even to this day' (1 Sam. 8:8).

The rule of Yahweh as king understandably became a particular focus of attention as Israel confronted her neighbours. In the polytheistic ancient Near East, conflicts between nations were regarded as conflicts between their gods, trials of strength like that on Mount Carmel (1 Kgs 18), but on an international scale. Thus we find in the Psalms that Yahweh is especially praised for his rule as King over other gods:

> For the LORD is a great God,
>   and a great King above all gods.
> (Ps. 95:3)

Yet in spite of his spectacular victories over other gods, it is still
his status as Creator that underlines the uniqueness of Yahweh.
Thus the psalmist immediately continues:

> In his hand are the depths of the earth;
>> the heights of the mountains are his also.
>
> (v. 4)

These themes of creation and rule over the nations are particularly
prominent in Isaiah:

> It is he who sits above the circle of the earth,
>> and its inhabitants are like grasshoppers;
> who stretches out the heavens like a curtain,
>> and spreads them like a tent to dwell in;
> who brings princes to nothing,
>> and makes the rulers of the earth as emptiness.
>
> (Isa. 40:22–23)

It is thus impossible to deny that God is king. However, it might
still be possible to question whether he should be conceived this
way in the doctrine of the atonement: perhaps here he should be
thought of as judge. Grotius himself retains the idea of God as
judge, and rightly so, as we have seen from John's Gospel. Jesus is,
to use Karl Barth's phrase (though without echoing his meaning)
the judge judged in our place.[9] Equally, though, Grotius is right
that God must be thought of as ruler. A judge who is not also a
king is a judge under the law. He is therefore not free to forgive a
sinner or to transfer punishment to someone else, for this is the
prerogative of a ruler, the one who promulgates the law. The
Reformed believe this no less than an Arminian like Grotius. John
Owen, for example, agrees that the transfer of punishment to
Christ was 'a relaxation of the law':

---

9. For an outline and critique of Barth's doctrine of the atonement, see
Williams 2008.

> It is true, indeed, there is a relaxation of the law in respect of the
> persons suffering, God admitting of commutation; as in the old law,
> when in their sacrifices the life of the beast was accepted (in respect to
> the carnal part of the ordinances) for the life of the man.
>
> (Owen 1967a: 173 [1.3])

Only a ruler, one over the law, may relax the requirement of the
law in this way. Hence, Owen insists several times in his *Dissertation
on Divine Justice* that 'God certainly does not punish us as being
injured, but as a ruler and judge' (Owen 1967b: 505 [1.2]). The
claim that punishment is transferred, a claim inherent to the penal
substitutionary doctrine, thus requires that we consider God in his
political role as ruler over the creation.

   The importance of having a double conception of God as ruler
and judge is also evident from the nature of theological language.
When we understand how God speaks of himself, we can see why
he is described by more than one term. Every term we use to
describe God carries with it similarities and differences from its
normal human usage. Thus when the Bible speaks of God as a
lion, a rock or dry rot, certain aspects of these descriptions are
applicable to God while others are not. The multiplicity of the
ways in which God speaks of himself allows the different terms to
regulate one another. In our example, God is at once like and unlike
human rulers, and human rulers are both similar to and different
from him. So too he is at once like and unlike human judges, and
human judges are both similar to and different from him. The use
of the terms 'ruler' and 'judge' alongside each other in the doctrine
of the atonement begins to show us which elements are to be
applied to God and which are not.

   In technical terms, the use of creaturely language for God is
neither *univocal* nor *equivocal*, but *analogical*. A term is used *univocally*
when it has exactly the same sense in one use as in another. Used
univocally, a term would have exactly the same meaning for God
as it has for one of his creatures. To claim that all our speech about
God is univocal would draw God and the creation too closely
together, resulting finally in pantheism. A term used *equivocally* has
a completely different sense in one use from another. Thus a term
used equivocally of God would have a totally different sense for

him from when it is used of a creature. To claim that all our speech of God is equivocal would render it impossible to speak about God at all, resulting finally in speechless mysticism or atheism. However, our speech about God is neither univocal nor equivocal, but *analogical*. That is, some aspects of a word's meaning are the same when it is used of God and of creatures, while others are different. Thomas Aquinas explains:

> Some things are said of God and creatures analogically, and not in a purely equivocal nor in a purely univocal sense. For we can name God only from creatures. Thus, whatever is said of God and creatures, is said according to the relation of a creature to God as its principle and cause, wherein all perfections pre-exist excellently.
>
> (Aquinas 1981, 1: 64 [1a.13.5])

Here Aquinas argues that words may be used of God analogically because we find within the creation the fingerprints, so to speak, of God: God has left his mark on creation, so that we can see in creatures lesser instantiations of the perfections of God. Goodness, for example, is found in creatures but has its source and original in God. Thus we can speak of God using a concept of goodness with which we are familiar, but we must remember that it is different in God. As Aquinas puts it, the statement 'God is good' means '*Whatever good we attribute to creatures, pre-exists in God,* and in a more excellent and higher way' (1: 61 [1a.13.2]).

Agreeing with Aquinas on this point does not automatically commit us to his doctrine of the *analogia entis* (analogy of being), which makes the quite distinct claim that the fingerprints of God in creation give us a basis for successful natural knowledge of God apart from special revelation. The doctrines of natural theology and the *analogia entis* are rightly rejected by Protestants, but the idea of analogical predication merely seeks to articulate, in the light of special revelation, how concepts from the world *can* be used to refer to God. It does not claim that we can know *how* they should be used to describe him apart from special revelation, nor even that we can know *that* they may be so used. This means that the point of contact between creation and God is present ontically because the being of the world reflects God, but it is broken epistemically

because of our sin: we would be blind to it apart from special revelation and illumination by the Holy Spirit.

One of the main reasons we need multiple concepts for understanding God is that he is in himself a wholly simple, unitary
being. He has no 'parts' he can lose: he is utterly indivisible. This
does not mean he is 'static' or 'lifeless', but rather in a unique way
he possesses all of his life at once and cannot lose or gain any of
it. He is maximally alive. Indeed his essence is to exist – he is the
self-existent 'I AM', who exists necessarily, which means he cannot
cease to be all he is, and therefore cannot lose any of his attributes
but rather is identical with each of them. By contrast, creatures are
compounded and divisible. Created things have 'parts' they can
lose; they do not exist necessarily; they experience the few proper-
ties they have in a fragmented manner. Consequently no single
created thing can ever serve fully to describe God. As Aquinas
puts it, 'the forms of the things whereof God is cause do not
attain to the species of the divine virtue, since they receive sever-
ally and particularly that which is in God simply and universally'
(Aquinas 1924–9, 1: 76 [1.32]).

This material from Aquinas is helpful in showing why we need
to think of God as both ruler and judge in the atonement. Taken
by itself, the idea of God as judge might be thought to suggest his
subordination to the law; thinking of God as ruler reminds us that
he is the sovereign giver of the law. Indeed it is likely in view of
God's simplicity that the proper description of any aspect of
special revelation will need to employ several creaturely concepts.
The concurrent affirmation of these concepts means they can regulate each other, and can combine to reflect more of the maximal
life of God.

The demonstration of divine justice in the atonement
We turn now to Grotius' second claim, that God acts in the atonement publicly to demonstrate his justice.

Trials scenes in Isaiah and John
There is extensive evidence within Scripture that God is concerned for the public demonstration of his justice. One strand of
evidence is found in Isaiah 40 – 55, where Yahweh summons

either Israel (42:18–25; 43:22–28; 50:1–3) or the nations (41:1–5;
41:21–29; 43:8–13; 44:6–8; 45:18–25) to appear before him in a
series of 'trial scenes'.[10] The people consistently fail to produce
their own witnesses against God, while Yahweh produces abundant evidence. Against his people he adduces his faithfulness, his
sovereign control over their plight, and their sin. Against the
nations he cites his unique deity, demonstrated especially in the
way he has ruled over and foretold events. As Lincoln argues, this
material from Isaiah provides an illuminating background against
which to read John's Gospel; indeed there is good reason to think
that John was written with these chapters of Isaiah consciously in
mind.

The connections are numerous. There are three quotations
from Isaiah in John (Isa. 40:3 in John 1:23; Isa. 53:1 in John 12:38;
and Isa. 54:13 in John 6:45). Lincoln explains that the location of
the first two at the start and finish of the public ministry of Jesus
forms an *inclusio*, flagging the significance of Isaiah 40 – 55 for
John's narrative (Lincoln 2000: 46). John also deploys many images
used by the prophet, including light (Isa. 42:6; John 9), the shepherd (Isa. 40:11; John 10) and water (Isa. 43:20; John 4:13–15;
7:37–39). Moreover, John contains specific links to Isaiah's trial
scenes. For example, the words *egō eimi* spoken on numerous occasions by Jesus in John are found in the Septuagint of Isaiah. As in
the Gospel, they are sometimes absolute and sometimes predicated (e.g. absolute in Isa. 41:4, predicated in Isa. 45:19). A number
of these occurrences are in the trial scenes (e.g. Isa. 41:4; 43:10, 25;
45:18, 19, 22), where they are often connected with God's ability to
predict the future, and in view of this it is noteworthy that Jesus
uses the absolute form in John 13:19, when he explains why he
predicted his betrayal: 'that when it does take place you may
believe that *egō eimi*'. Jesus uses the divine name again when he is
arrested to be tried before Annas and Pilate, who represent Israel
and the nations (18:5–6). Finally, just as Isaiah records Yahweh's
insistence that he 'did not speak in secret, / in a land of darkness'

(Isa. 45:19), so also Jesus points to the public character of his ministry during his trial: 'I have said nothing in secret' (John 18:20).

Public crucifixion

The fact that the Lord Jesus died by crucifixion also supports the claim that in the atonement God was concerned to demonstrate his justice publicly. Crucifixion was a favoured means of execution in the ancient world precisely because of its very public character: it openly exhibited the 'justice' and power of the Roman Empire. According to the first-century rhetorician Quintilian, this explained the choice of location for crucifixions: 'Whenever we crucify the guilty, the most crowded roads are chosen, where the most people can see and be moved by this fear' (*Declamations*, 274, cited in Hengel 1977: 50 n. 14). The emperor Justinian's *Digest of Roman Law* made this intention explicit: 'That the sight may deter others from such crimes and be a comfort to the relatives and neighbours of those whom they have killed, the penalty is to be exacted in the place where the robbers did their murders' (*Digest*, 48.19.28.15, cited in Hengel 1977: 50). Similarly Josephus records that during the siege of Jerusalem, Titus commiserated with the fate of the 500 or more Jews who were crucified every day, but allowed the crucifixions to continue in 'the hope that the spectacle might perhaps induce the Jews to surrender, for fear that continued resistance would involve them in a similar fate' (Josephus 1968, 3: 341 [5.450]).

The nakedness of the crucified

Those condemned to crucifixion were normally stripped naked, and this would have further emphasized Jesus' public humiliation. Alfred Edersheim points out that the Jews kept at least a bare minimum of clothing on those they executed by stoning, and on this basis argues that 'every concession would be made to Jewish custom, and hence we thankfully believe that on the Cross He was spared the indignity of exposure' (Edersheim 1897, 2: 584). This unusual procedure might have occurred, but in view of the insensitivity to Jewish concerns expressed in Pilate's refusal to change the title over the cross, it seems distinctly unlikely. It is much more likely that Jesus was crucified naked, in the usual Roman fashion.

Melito of Sardis, writing in the second century, believed that Christ was naked, and even used this to explain the darkness over the land:

> O unprecedented murder! Unprecedented crime!
> The Sovereign has been made unrecognizable by his naked body,
> and is not even allowed a garment to keep him from view.
> That is why the luminaries turned away,
> and the day was darkened,
> so that he might hide the one stripped bare upon the tree,
> darkening not the body of the Lord
> but the eyes of men.
> (Melito of Sardis 1979: 55 [97])

Nakedness has great significance in Scripture. After the expulsion from Eden, nakedness is widely identified with sin and its public punishment. For example, Jeremiah warns Jerusalem that she will be exposed publicly for her prostitution: 'I myself will lift up your skirts over your face, and your shame will be seen. I have seen your abominations, your adulteries and neighings, your lewd harlotries, on the hills in the field' (13:26–27; cf. v. 22). Again, Lamentations connects the nakedness of the drunken daughter of Edom with the punishment of her sin:

> Rejoice and be glad, O daughter of Edom,
>   you who dwell in the land of Uz;
> but to you also the cup shall pass;
>   you shall become drunk and strip yourself bare (*wĕtit'ārî*).
>
> The punishment of your iniquity, O daughter of Zion, is accomplished;
>   he will keep you in exile no longer;
> but your iniquity, O daughter of Edom, he will punish;
>   he will uncover (*gillâ*) your sins.
> (4:21–22)

The verbs used here are different, but the connection between nakedness in sin and in punishment is clear because the second verb (*glh*, in the piel) can have the same sense of physical nakedness or exposure as the first. Similarly Hosea warns Israel that her nakedness in adultery will be met with nakedness as she is stripped in punishment:

> Plead with your mother, plead –
>   for she is not my wife,
>   and I am not her husband –
> that she put away her whoring from her face,
>   and her adultery from between her breasts;
> lest I strip her naked
>   and make her as in the day she was born,
> and make her like a wilderness,
>   and make her like a parched land,
>   and kill her with thirst.
> (Hos. 2:2–3)

The pattern of double nakedness is later applied by Ezekiel to Jerusalem herself. Just as she has exposed herself and played the harlot with the nations, Yahweh will now gather the nations and expose her before them, and they will attack and strip her:

> Thus says the Lord GOD, Because your lust was poured out and your nakedness uncovered in your whorings with your lovers, and with all your abominable idols, and because of the blood of your children that you gave to them, therefore, behold, I will gather all your lovers with whom you took pleasure, all those you loved and all those you hated; I will gather them against you from every side and will uncover your nakedness to them, that they may see all your nakedness.. . . And I will give you into their hands, and they shall throw down your vaulted chamber and break down your lofty places; they shall strip you of your clothes and take your beautiful jewels and leave you naked and bare.
>
> (Ezek. 16:36–37, 39)

Standing naked before the nations is therefore a sign of divine punishment for Israel and Judah. The Lord Jesus, the New Israel, stood in the place of his people and was stripped naked for them, bearing in his own body their public judgment and punishment.

Romans 3:25–26

Finally, the importance of the public character of the atonement as the demonstration of divine justice is established by the words of the apostle Paul. In Romans 3 Paul explains why God set forth the Lord Jesus as a propitiation for sins:

> This was to show God's righteousness (*eis endeixin tēs dikaiosynēs autou*), because in his divine forbearance he had passed over former sins. It was to show his righteousness at the present time (*pros tēn endeixin tēs dikaiosynēs autou en tō nun kairō*), so that he might be just and the justifier of the one who has faith in Jesus.
>
> (3:25–26)

God publicly demonstrated his 'righteousness (*dikaiosynē*)' in the cross. The meaning of this term is disputed. In particular, it is often denied that it denotes God's distributive justice (*iustitia distributiva*); rather, it is claimed, God's *dikaiosynē* is his covenant faithfulness. John Ziesler comments that it is 'likely that God's righteousness here has its usual Pauline saving connotations, and so does not mean his strict justice of the "eye for an eye" sort, but his action to restore and maintain the divine–human relationship' (Ziesler 1989: 115). The affirmation here is true, but the denial trades on a false dichotomy between God's covenant faithfulness and his punitive justice, a dichotomy that misunderstands the nature of the covenant relationship itself as it is fulfilled in the work of Christ.

Certainly righteousness in Paul is God's saving righteousness. But to think that the righteousness demonstrated at the cross cannot therefore also be his retribution against sin is to fail to understand how the covenant operates. God's covenant faithfulness is both his faithfulness in saving his chosen people and his faithfulness in executing the covenant curses against those who have broken it. The insight that *dikaiosynē* is covenant faithfulness (God restoring the 'divine–human relationship') actually *requires* us to recognize that the atonement involved punishing sin to remove the curse that stood against Israel. Thus at the cross God did not pass over sin, but rather revealed his saving, punishing righteousness, proving that he is indeed righteous, both in the sense that he punishes and in the sense that he saves. The justice of God that had been in question was demonstrated for all to see.

Colossians 2:11–15

In Colossians 2 Paul testifies to the public nature of the cross. Reading Christ's death as a kind of circumcision, Paul explains that the Colossians have been circumcised in Christ. The analogy may not seem obvious to us, but the links are real: both circumcision and the cross are instances of covenant-forming by blood-shedding. Having identified circumcision with the death of Christ, Paul then makes a similar link to baptism: in baptism the believer dies and rises with Christ as he believes in God's work. Thus the spiritually dead and uncircumcised are forgiven and made alive (Col. 2:13). At this point Paul picks up on this act of forgiveness and explains how it has been accomplished: God has cancelled the legal bond (*cheirographon*) 'which stood against us with its legal demands (*tois dogmasin*)' (v. 14). It was erased by being nailed to the cross, a reference to the fact that the nailing of Christ to the cross erased the debt, possibly with a further allusion to the *titulus* (inscription) over the cross: 'God nails the accusation against us to the cross of Jesus, just as his accusation had been nailed there' (O'Brien 1982: 126).

Here is a forensic description of the atonement: the legal curse is borne by Christ. In doing this, God achieved his victory: God is victor because Christ has borne the curse. There is no need to see a change of subject here from God to Christ if we read the verb *apekdyomai* (literally 'undressing') as active in sense and take it to mean 'disarming'. It is not that Christ strips himself of the clinging powers (making him the subject), but that God disarms them. This also allows us to read the final *en autō* (v. 15) as a reference to Christ, continuing the sustained theme of union with Christ found in the repeated use of the expression in this section and in the recurring use of verbs with the *syn-* prefix. Thus God achieved his victory in Christ. The forensic work of Christ is the ground of his victory: penal substitution here explains Christus Victor. By means of Christ's forensic work God disarmed the spiritual 'principalities and powers (*tas archas kai tas exousias*)' and, having disarmed them, shamed them in public (*edeigmatisen en parrēsia*).

The language of 'shaming' found here alludes to a Roman tri-
umphal procession, the celebration of a returning conqueror with
all his spoils and victims displayed before him. Plutarch gives us a
sense of the kind of occasion when he records the triumph of
Aemilius Paullus, the Roman general who defeated Perseus, king
of Macedonia, in the Third Macedonian War at the battle of
Pydna (168 BC). The description goes into considerable detail, but
it is the treatment of Perseus himself that shows the depths of
humiliation reached by the defeated:

> Behind the children and their retinue came Perseus. He wore a grey cloak
> and Macedonian boots, and looked as though he was utterly astounded
> and bewildered by the magnitude of the disaster that had happened to
> him. He too was accompanied by a crowd of associates and friends; their
> faces were heavy with grief, but because they were constantly glancing at
> Perseus and weeping they gave the spectators to understand that they
> were mourning his fate and did not care in the slightest for their own.
> Perseus had written to Aemilius, asking not to be paraded through the
> streets and included in the triumph, but Aemilius, apparently in mockery
> of Perseus' cowardice and fear of death, remarked: 'The situation is no
> different now from what it was before: he could grant his own request,
> if he wanted.' He meant that he could always choose death instead of
> dishonour, but the coward could not bring himself to do that. Instead,
> unmanned by hope, he became a part of his own spoils.
>
> (Plutarch 1999: 71–72 [34])

In alluding to such a spectacle, the apostle Paul shows that he saw
the cross as a public victory. In so far as Grotius emphasized that
God is a ruler concerned to demonstrate his legally just victory in
public, he was in step with Paul.

Summary

After surveying some historical and biblical evidence for the integration of political concepts and the doctrine of the cross, we have
examined two examples of such integration in the teaching of
Grotius: God as ruler in the doctrine of the atonement, and the
public demonstration of divine justice at the cross. Each claim, considered in isolation from other elements of the Grotian doctrine,

rests on good biblical evidence. In neither case is the doctrine of the atonement corrupted by political language and concepts; on the contrary, these concepts illuminate the doctrine and secure important elements within it.

Part 2: from the cross to the public square

The charge

We now approach the cross and politics from the second angle, considering not the use of concepts from the public square to illuminate the cross, but reflecting upon the deployment of the doctrine of the cross in the public square. It is sometimes claimed that such an enterprise is impossible. For example Weaver maintains that penal substitution 'is an a-ethical atonement image – it projects an understanding of salvation that is separated from ethics' (Weaver 2005: 49). If he is right, then we should be deeply troubled, for Christian ethics is not some ancillary discipline worked out long after the gospel has been forgotten; it is the organic efflorescence of the gospel in the life of the Christian and the church. Reformed theology has long integrated doctrine and ethics. Karl Barth, for example, even though he departed from historic Reformed theology in many ways, saw the importance of preserving this connection in regard to the atonement: 'In Christian ethics . . . the atonement made in Jesus Christ cannot simply be a presupposition which has been left far behind' (Barth 1956: 101).

Indeed Weaver goes even further in arguing that penal substitutionary atonement is not merely ethically useless, but is actually harmful: it is unethical, since it subverts faithful Christian living. For Weaver, the satisfaction theory is the source of 'the centuries-long use of Christian theology to accommodate violence both systemic and direct' (Weaver 2001: 225). Ironically, then, while some evangelicals fear that engagement in the public square may lead them away from their own theology, their critics maintain that precisely by maintaining their theology evangelicals have already endorsed the worst elements of culture. All was well with Christian theology, the critics declare, until Constantine was converted; only then did people begin believing in such wicked notions as penal substitution, which led in turn to child abuse, patriarchy, oppression, torture and the death penalty.[11] The problem, according to Weaver and Vic Thiessen, is that penal substitution moves God too close to the action of the cross, identifying him with, and thus legitimating the actions of, the oppressors of Jesus and their successors. Indeed, according to Thiessen, this conclusion is unavoidable: 'No matter how you interpret the satisfaction theory of the atonement, you cannot get away from the basic fact that in this theory God was the arranger and therefore author of Jesus' death' (Thiessen 2005: 41).

Weaver's alternative

Anabaptist theologians like Weaver and Thiessen are concerned, therefore, to diminish the agency of God in Christ's death, so that he cannot be seen in any way to legitimate such a horror as crucifixion. The corollary of this is an increased isolation of, and emphasis upon, the resurrection as *the* saving event. Indeed, in his doctrine of 'narrative Christus Victor', Weaver even affirms on several occasions the soteriological significance of the resurrection at the expense of the cross. Since this may seem hard to believe, I provide several examples:

> In narrative Christus Victor, the death of Jesus is anything but a loving act of God; it is the product of the forces of evil that oppose the reign of God.
>
> (Weaver 2001: 45)

> This contrast of Jesus' death as *needed* and *not needed* indicates one of the most profound differences between narrative Christus Victor and satisfaction atonement.
>
> (72)

> The agent of Jesus' death was not God but the powers of evil.
>
> (74)

---

11. This is a common theme in the work of Stuart Murray, e.g. S. Murray 2005.

God did not need the death of Jesus.

(Weaver 2005: 57)

This suffering is not something willed by nor needed by God and it is not directed Godward. On the contrary, the killing of Jesus is the ultimate contrast between the non-violent reign of God and the rule of evil.

(57)

The real saving act of and in and with Jesus is his resurrection.

(57)

Rather than the death of Jesus, what sinners need, what the reign of God needs, is the resurrection of Jesus. That is where the victory of the reign of God is.

(58)[12]

There is a dynamic connection here between the different aspects of Weaver's position. The central charge is that penal substitution fosters abuse by identifying God as the cause of Christ's suffering at Calvary. From this it follows that God must be distanced from the cross to avoid mandating evil human practices. For this reason the decisive act of salvation must be located elsewhere, in an event which can safely be attributed to God, namely Christ's resurrection. The characterization is plain: the resurrection was the saving work of God, but the crucifixion was merely an act of evil men.

Critique of Weaver
The compulsion driving the Anabaptist position is clear: the action of God must be moved from the cross to the resurrection to avoid legitimating victimization and suffering. Before addressing the criticism of penal substitution itself, it is worth pausing to consider whether this alternative soteriological schema might be viable. Four major difficulties stand out, suggesting that it is not.

---

12. The same point is made in the same volume in Northcott 2005: 94.

Internal inconsistency
First, the claim that the cross was somehow unnecessary for God's plan of salvation cannot stand even within Weaver's system. Indeed Weaver himself takes a small step toward this conclusion in his acknowledgment that the cross was 'the inevitable result' of Jesus' mission (Weaver 2001: 132). For Weaver, this does not mean that God needed the cross; it was merely the unintended 'result of pursuing another goal', namely to make known the reign of God (133). But Weaver's position implies more than this. If the resurrection was always God's intended means of triumphing over the depths of evil, then the death of Christ was not just the inevitable but also the necessary prelude to the great saving event itself. To use the terminology favoured by Anabaptist writers, if the evil had not been poured out on Jesus, then it could not have been absorbed by him and defeated. Evil must be evoked before it can be engaged. If God intended the resurrection when he sent his Son, he must also have intended the cross.

The only way to avoid this conclusion would be to posit another goal for the life of Jesus apart from his resurrection, perhaps simply the goal of making known the reign of God. Then one might say that God did not intend the death of his Son, and that, taken by surprise at Calvary, he raised Christ triumphantly from the dead. On this model the cross was not intended, but neither was the resurrection. This compromises still further God's foreknowledge and purposefulness, and is thus even harder to square with the biblical data. In summary, the attempt to remove the cross from the purpose of God cannot stand even on its own terms, unless we are willing to say that God did not intend to save by the resurrection either. If he willed to save by the resurrection, then in some significant sense he willed the cross.

God wills the cross
Second, the Scriptures emphasize that God willed the cross. In Isaiah we read that God willed the suffering of his Servant: 'the LORD has laid on him / the iniquity of us all', and 'it was the will of the LORD to crush him' (53:6, 10). In the New Testament, Jesus is identified as the Servant who is crushed by the Lord (e.g. 1 Pet. 2:21–24). This interpretation finds confirmation from the lips of

Jesus when he quotes Zechariah 13:7 on the night of his betrayal:
'Jesus said to them, "You will all fall away, for it is written, 'I
will strike the shepherd, and the sheep will be scattered'"' (Mark
14:27; cf. Matt. 26:31). Interestingly the Gospels emphasize that it
is God himself who does this. Whereas the Hebrew and the
Septuagint contain a second person imperative, addressed to
Yahweh's sword ('Awake, O sword . . . Strike'), the Gospels have
the first person future, *pataxō* (I will strike), emphasizing God's
personal involvement rather than the more impersonal image of
the sword.[13]

Further evidence that God intended the cross may be found in
Acts. After their release by the Jewish leaders, Peter and John
gather with their friends and praise God, proclaiming in prayer
that Herod and Pilate gathered together against Jesus 'with the
Gentiles and the peoples of Israel, to do whatever your hand and
your plan had predestined to take place' (Acts 4:27–28). Thus in a
prayer addressing the 'Sovereign Lord' (*despota*, v. 24), the apostles
explicitly affirm exactly what Weaver denies. Even Christopher
Marshall, who is very sympathetic to Weaver's proposals, judges
that denials of God willing the cross and of its necessity 'fly in the
face of the accumulated weight of New Testament evidence'
(Marshall 2003: 81).

Jesus died 'for our transgressions'
Third, the Bible teaches that the Lord Jesus died not just 'for us'
but 'for our trespasses (*dia ta paraptōmata hēmōn*)' (Rom. 4:25).
Weaver can explain that Jesus died 'for *us*' in the sense of 'for our
benefit', for he claims that Jesus' death revealed the evil of the
powers that held us (Weaver 2001: 75–76). But the fact that Christ
died 'for *our transgressions*' poses insuperable problems for Weaver's
scheme. The preposition *dia* with the accusative can convey one of
two senses, indicating either an antecedent cause ('because of our

---

13. The Hebrew reads *hak* (hiphil imperative masculine singular of *nkh*), the
Septuagint *pataxate* (second person plural aorist imperative active of
patassō), and the New Testament *pataxō* (first person singular future
indicative active of *patassō*).

trespasses') or a final cause ('for the sake of our trespasses').[14] Clearly Paul cannot intend a final cause here: Christ's death was not 'for the sake of' our trespasses, or 'with a view to' them. But what sense could Weaver make of the statement that Christ died 'because of our trespasses'? His only option would be to claim that Jesus died 'because of our trespasses' in the sense that we killed Jesus, for we were enslaved by the powers that killed him. Weaver hints at such a view in comments like this:

> Being a sinner means to acknowledge our identification with those who killed Jesus and our bondage to the powers that enslaved them. Every human being, by virtue of what human society is, participates in and is in bondage to those powers and is therefore implicated in the killing of Jesus.
>
> (2001: 75; cf. 216)

The supposed logic here is clear: the powers killed Jesus; we are enslaved to the powers; therefore we killed Jesus. Hence Weaver might say, Jesus died 'because of our trespasses' in that we shared in the trespass of killing him. But there is simply no logic in this argument. Putting it simply, I was not alive when Jesus was killed. Others sinned in killing him; I did not. He might have died 'because of' the sin of the Sanhedrin, but he did not die because of my sin. He might even have died because of *my kind* of sin, in that my sin is like that of the Sanhedrin, but he did not die because of *my* sin. By contrast, Reformed theology can speak of Jesus dying because of my trespasses, because God reckoned them to be his on the grounds of the union between Christ and his people.

The cross saves
Fourth, the statements made by these writers diminish the saving role of the cross, which Scripture unashamedly magnifies. Again and again, we read that the cross justifies, reconciles, delivers,

---

14. On the preposition, see Robertson 1919: 583–584. Very occasionally there is a spatial sense, e.g. Luke 17:11. On the meaning of the preposition in Rom. 4:25, see e.g. Moo 1996: 289.

redeems, makes peace, defeats and destroys the devil, purifies from
and puts away sin, and brings us to God (e.g. Rom. 5:9–10; Gal.
1:4; 3:13; Eph. 1:7; Col. 1:20; 2:13–14; Tit. 2:14; Heb. 2:14–15; 9:26;
1 Pet. 3:18). Indeed even Weaver's own affirmation of 'narrative
Christus Victor' undermines his disavowal of the saving effect of
the cross, for according to Hebrews 2:14–15 it was the death of
Christ that defeated the devil. Indeed this was the very purpose
of the incarnation:

> Since therefore the children share in flesh and blood, he himself likewise
> partook of the same things, that through death he might destroy the one
> who has the power of death, that is, the devil, and deliver all those who
> through fear of death were subject to lifelong slavery.
>
> (2:14–15)[15]

Weaver affirms that the Lamb triumphs in the resurrection, but
(contra Hebrews) he denies that Christ conquers as the *slain*
Lamb. Weaver may cry 'Christus Victor!' but Scripture proclaims
'Christus Victor!' of the Lamb qua *agnus qui occisus est* (the lamb
who was slain).

This is not to deny the resurrection its place in the victory of
Christ. Whereas Weaver locates salvation in the resurrection and
not in the cross, we must locate it in both. What Weaver sunders,
we must join together. Calvin makes this point well when he
explains how Scripture speaks synecdochically of the cross and the
resurrection: 'whenever (*quoties*) mention is made of his death
alone, we are to understand at the same time what belongs to his
resurrection', and vice versa (Calvin 1960, 1: 521 [2.16.13]; the Latin
is from Calvin 1834, 1: 337). Perhaps *quoties* is an overstatement,
but generally the point stands. While we must recognize the roles
of human agents in the suffering of the Lord Jesus, Scripture prohibits us from ascribing the cross exclusively to men and denying
its saving role (it does not of course prohibit ascribing the resurrection exclusively to God). We cry 'Christus Victor!' of both the

---

15. Weaver cites these verses without noting that they locate the victory at a
different point from his own scheme (Weaver 2001: 64).

cross and the resurrection, identifying both his sin-bearing and his resurrection-justification as victory.

Anyone for bridge?

Having demonstrated that the Anabaptist construction cannot stand, it is now necessary to demonstrate that penal substitutionary atonement does not fall prey to the criticisms levelled at it. The literature on this question resembles something like a game of bridge, with each side attempting to trump the other in successive rounds. The Anabaptists lead with a proponent of penal substitutionary atonement who was involved in what they regard as immoral action, perhaps Calvin and the execution of Servetus. Advocates of penal substitution follow suit, citing examples of believers in penal substitution who were renowned for their public virtue, such as William Wilberforce or Lord Shaftesbury. The Anabaptists then change suits, leading with an instance of a connection between penal substitutionary atonement and what they consider to be unacceptable political theory, for example Martin Luther's theological endorsement of the treatment of the peasants in the Peasants' War. Proponents of penal substitution follow suit again, perhaps citing the impetus for resistance against unlawful tyrants provided by Reformed political theorists, for example in the *Vindiciae, Contra Tyrannos* or the *Politica* of Johannes Althusius. And so the game proceeds.

Unlike bridge itself, this exercise is pointless. Anyone with some knowledge of history can cite numerous outstanding examples on both sides. Moreover, in every instance, alternative explanations of both the good and the bad are possible that have nothing to do with the doctrine of the atonement, such as Luther's fear of disorder or the Reformed desire to authorize rebellion in order to preserve their own religion. The fallen human mind is capable of twisting any doctrine, whether true or false, to provide an excuse for sin. Penal substitutionary atonement is hardly unique in this respect.

Flawed historical reconstructions

Nonetheless, since some critics have opened the bidding, it is necessary to point out that some of their historical reconstructions are flawed. Two examples will suffice. First, Stuart Murray and others have claimed that the conversion of Constantine resulted in the demise of the idea of Christus Victor because the church was no longer in conflict with the world and therefore no longer sought solace in the victory of Christ. An accepted church needed a new, more authority-affirming model of atonement rather than one that located authority outside the state in Christ. As Murray puts it, '*Christus Victor* was much less appealing now that Christians were no longer on the margins and a "Christian empire" might conceivably be one of the oppressive powers from which the death of Jesus offered salvation!' (S. Murray 2005: 31).

But this reconstruction of the reason for the move away from Christus Victor is without historical foundation, since there is no evidence that Constantine renounced the emphasis on Christ's victory. On the contrary, he favoured an understanding of the cross as conquest precisely because he was a conquering Christian emperor.[16] It is utterly bizarre to think that the emperor given victory by Christ should have found the idea of Christ's victory uncomfortable. Constantine did not leave the idea of victory behind; he embraced it under a new identity, turning from Sol Invictus (the Unconquered Sun) to Christus Victor, a move made easier by the biblical description of the Messiah as the 'sun of righteousness' (Mal. 4:2).

The cross is repeatedly associated with the language of conquest and victory in Eusebius' account of Constantine's conversion in *The Life of Constantine*. Eusebius records the sworn description he received from 'the victorious emperor' after his victory over Maxentius: 'He said that about noon, when the day was already beginning to decline, he saw with his own eyes the trophy of a cross of light in the heavens, above the sun, and bearing the inscription, CONQUER BY THIS' (Eusebius 1995: 490 [1.28]). When Constantine sought an explanation of the sign, it came clothed in the language of victory: it was the sign of the Son of God, 'the symbol of immortality, and the trophy of that victory over death which He had gained in time past when sojourning on

---

16. For an exploration of this point, see Gillman 1961. This material is
    deployed against Weaver in Boersma 2004: 157–158.

earth' (491 [1.32]). The emperor then marched against the armies
of Maxentius with this sign of Christus Victor as his emblem:

> Assuming therefore the Supreme God as his patron, and invoking His
> Christ to be his preserver and aid, and setting the victorious trophy, the
> salutary symbol, in front of his soldiers and body-guard, he marched
> with his whole forces, trying to obtain again for the Romans the freedom
> they had inherited from their ancestors.
>
> (492 [1.37])

After taking Rome itself, Constantine memorialized his victory
with a statue that continued to exhibit the victorious cross:

> By loud proclamation and monumental inscriptions he made known to
> all men the salutary symbol, setting up this great trophy of victory over
> his enemies in the midst of the imperial city, and expressly causing it to
> be engraven in indelible characters, that the salutary symbol was the
> safeguard of the Roman government and of the entire empire.
> Accordingly, he immediately ordered a lofty spear in the figure of a cross
> to be placed beneath the hand of a statue representing himself, in the
> most frequented part of Rome, and the following inscription to be
> engraved on it in the Latin language: BY VIRTUE OF THIS SALUTARY SIGN,
> WHICH IS THE TRUE TEST OF VALOR, I HAVE PRESERVED AND LIBERATED
> YOUR CITY FROM THE YOKE OF TYRANNY. I HAVE ALSO SET AT LIBERTY THE
> ROMAN SENATE AND PEOPLE, AND RESTORED THEM TO THEIR ANCIENT
> DISTINCTION AND SPLENDOR.
>
> (493 [1.40])

Unlike Murray, Constantine and Eusebius saw no need to move
away from the idea of the cross as a victory. On the contrary, this
is precisely how Constantine understood the cross in the very
event to which Eusebius traced the emperor's conversion and
to which modern historians commonly trace the origin of
Christendom itself.

A second example of flawed historical reconstruction concerns
Anselm. In this case, we are told by Weaver, the intrusion of violence into theology that began with the conversion of the emperor
advanced toward its apogee in the medieval period:

> Narrative Christus Victor disappeared from the picture when the church
> came to support the world's social order, to accept the intervention of
> political authorities in churchly affairs, and to look to political authorities
> for support and protection.
>
> (2001: 88)

It is clear that Weaver is referring here to Anselm's own times:

> Anselm wrote in a time when church was assumed to encompass the
> social order, and God's providence (the reign of God) was assumed to
> be expressed through the course of the social order. Thus in Anselm's
> imagery, with the social order under control of God and no longer
> confronted by the church, it is quite understandable how Anselm's
> imagery deals only with components of the sin of individuals and does
> not deal with the structural (systemic) dimensions of sin.
>
> (88–89)

This is a somewhat surprising characterization of the context in
which Anselm lived and wrote.[17] Anselm was consecrated as
Archbishop of Canterbury in 1093, by which time he had already
clashed with the king, William Rufus, over control of the land and
tenants he held as Archbishop. The dispute intensified when
Anselm wanted to go to Rome to receive his pallium from the
Pope, Urban II.[18] William did not initially recognize Urban as
Pope, and three times refused Anselm permission to go. In the end
Anselm left without permission and was able to return only after
William's death. By then, the Council of Rome (1099) had decided
against the possibility of lay investiture (the appointment of clergy
by a lay ruler). On returning to England, Anselm made his alle-
giance to the council's conclusions clear to the new king, Henry I,
and the controversy resumed.

In 1103 it was agreed that Anselm should go to Rome with a
royal messenger to discuss ways of preserving the honour of the

---

17. The biographical details that follow are from Evans 1989: ch. 1.
18. A pallium is a distinctive woollen vestment granted by the Pope to arch-
    bishops.

king. The Pope held out against the king's claims, and Anselm remained in exile until 1107. In the light of these basic facts of Anselmian biography, it can hardly be claimed that at this time the church came 'to accept the intervention of political authorities in churchly affairs', and the social order was 'no longer confronted by the church'.

The inner logic of the cross

A more authentic way to address the ethical consequences of penal substitutionary atonement is to examine the inner logic of the doctrine itself in its systematic context. When it is handled carefully, according to its own inner logic and the doctrines that relate to it, does penal substitution lend any support to unethical behaviour? Specifically how can we maintain that God willed the death of Jesus *without* mandating violence in the public square? Can we go further, to see how penal substitutionary atonement might have positive ethical implications when understood within its proper dogmatic context?

Defining violence

First, we must take care over our definition of violence. Clearly if we define violence simply as the infliction of some kind of pain on a person, then (with the vital qualification that the pain is voluntarily received by God himself in Christ) penal substitutionary atonement ascribes violence to God. This is the definition chosen by Weaver, who understands violence simply as 'harm or damage' (2001: 8). But such a bland definition of violence will not do, since it pays no attention to the grounds on which the pain is inflicted (the meritorious cause), or to its intended results (the final cause). According to this definition, I would be guilty of 'violence' if I injured someone while preventing them from falling under a moving train.

Weaver seeks to avoid this problem by distinguishing 'violence defined as harm or damage from non-violence as force or social coercion that respects bodily integrity'. Thus for Weaver 'violence' is inflicted at the moment when 'bodily integrity' is not respected. But this is still inadequate, because it does not explain how acts of psychological force that respect bodily integrity can still be violent, as they clearly are. As Hans Boersma comments, 'insistence on absolute nonviolence is often based on an arbitrary understanding of violence as something physical, so that we are willing to accept our involvement in other forms of coercion and force that often are no less invasive' (Boersma 2004: 44).

This is a very serious difficulty with Weaver's model of non-violent atonement. The internal inconsistency emerges in some of his own vocabulary. Describing the path of non-violent resistance advocated by the Lord Jesus, Weaver says that the oppressed person 'has the potential to seize the initiative, shame the offender, and strip him of the power to dehumanize'. Seizing, shaming and stripping: hardly the vocabulary of non-violence!

Again, Weaver's inability to expunge the idea of violence from his system emerges when we consider the place of Jesus' resurrection in his soteriology. The evil powers killed Jesus, but God triumphed over them by raising him from the dead. In doing this, God inflicted defeat on the powers by reversing what they had done. God seizes the initiative, shames them in public, and strips them of their power. Was this not a painful experience for the murderers of Jesus? Did it not inflict extreme frustration and mental suffering on them? Apart from the absence of bodily force, it is hard to see how the resurrection of Jesus, even on Weaver's terms, is non-violent. And if the absence of bodily force alone makes it non-violent, then extreme non-bodily psychological abuse is thereby excused. Thus, unless we focus exclusively on bodily harm in a way that gives licence to psychological harm, we must conclude that God is violent toward those who murdered Jesus. For this reason Hans Boersma, among others, rightly argues that we must retain the vocabulary of divine violence, recognizing that such violence is a good.

Divine and human action

This definition of violence points us to a crucial distinction, missed by these critics of penal substitution, between divine and human action in the history of the cross. Weaver thinks that because penal substitutionary atonement ascribes the action of the cross to God, it must ascribe the violence of the cross, considered as wrongful violence, to God. But this has never been maintained by proponents of penal substitution. Rather within Augustinian–Reformed theology, penal substitutionary atonement has been formulated alongside a strong commitment to the doctrine of divine providence, which provides a basis for distinguishing the action of God from the action of sinners in the death of Jesus. We have seen that Scripture requires us to ascribe the crucifixion of Jesus both to God and to sinful human beings: it was the Lord's will, and it was also an act for which Satan and men were morally responsible. The Reformed doctrine of providence shows us how we can maintain both assertions rather than following Weaver and sacrificing one to the other.

For an outline of this doctrine we turn to Benedict Pictet, one of the clearest and most concise Reformed Scholastic theologians. Pictet states the exhaustive scope of divine providence: 'Nothing is so contingent or accidental as not to fall under the Providence of God' (Pictet 1834: 162 [3.9]). There are according to Pictet two acts or operations of divine providence. The first is *preservation*, which is necessary because no creature can exist of itself: all things are upheld by God. The second is *government*, 'which is that operation of the divine will, by which he wisely orders all things' 165 [3.9]).

In his discussion of government, Pictet clarifies that God actually causes all things that occur; he does not confer some independent power on the creature by which the creature then acts. Rather God concurs in every action:

> We must not conceive the operation of God in concurring, and the
> operation of the second cause which admits that concurrence, to be two
> different actions, like those of two persons who draw the same rope. On
> the contrary, the operation or motion which is produced by the first cause
> in the second, is the same with the operation of the second cause – they
> are one and the same.
>
> (166 [3.9])

This may seem to make our difficulty all the more acute: if God is the cause of all things in such a strong sense, then how can we distinguish his action from the action of Pilate? Pictet is of course aware of this issue; he affirms that the liberty of the creature is not destroyed by divine government, and devotes another section to exploring how God relates to evil actions.

Explaining that God is not the author of sin, Pictet distinguishes between the *beginning, progress* and *end* of sin. The greater
part of his attention is focused on the *beginning*. He asserts that
God acts in five ways with regard to the beginning of sin: (1) he
permits it (e.g. Acts 14:16); (2) he gives sinners up to their sins (e.g.
Rom. 1:24, 26, 28); (3) he presents objects to the sinner that are
not in themselves sinful but which the sinner turns to sin (e.g.
Bathsheba being visible to David); (4) he allows Satan to assault
the sinner (Eph. 2:2); and (5) he stirs up thoughts in sinners that
are themselves good but may be turned to evil (e.g. Joseph's brothers thinking that their father loved Joseph).

At this point Pictet is aware that a more difficult question
remains, for some biblical texts appear actually to ascribe evil acts
to God. Pictet cites the biblical statements that God hardened
Pharaoh's heart (e.g. Exod. 9:12) and sent a lying spirit to Ahab (1
Kgs 22), and asks 'Whether God does anything more in respect to
sin, than what we have already laid down?' (173 [3.11]). Pictet
expresses some puzzlement at the exact meaning of such verses,
but then outlines the interpretation given by most divines: 'God is
the author of the essence of human actions, by virtue of his concurrence in producing them, but not the author of their sinfulness'
(173 [3.11]). By this Pictet means that any individual act may have
two causes, so that God may be the cause of the action regarded as
an action, but the sinner is the responsible cause of the action with
respect to its moral character. Francis Turretin makes the same
point:

> Although the premotion of God is extended to evil actions, it does not
> on that account make God guilty of the fault or the author of sin. It
> only pertains to actions inasmuch as they are material and entitative
> (*entitative*), not however as they are moral, i.e., to the substance of the act,
> but not to its wickedness.
>
> (Turretin 1992–7, 1: 509 [6.5.16])

Or again: 'the evil intention of man is not from God in the genus
of morals, but only in the genus of being' (527 [6.7.33]).

Pictet illustrates the distinction in the following way. Imagine a
man with a problem in his limbs that causes difficulty in walking.

The man's soul sends instructions to his limbs to walk normally,
yet he walks with his usual limp. Both the soul and the limbs are
causes of the walking, but the limbs alone, not the soul, are the
cause of the problem. In drawing a series of further distinc-
tions Pictet sheds more light on this idea of double causation. For
example, we may distinguish between an affection in itself (caused
by God) and the end toward which the affection is directed (caused
by the sinner):

> In order that hatred of God may be stirred up within the mind, certain
> motions must be previously stirred up in the body, and also certain
> thoughts in the soul, by which it is inclined to hate any object which may
> be presented to it. These motions and thoughts are not at all evil of
> themselves, but that direction of them toward God, which takes place by
> our own will, is the greatest of all sins (hatred of God).
>
> (Pictet 1834: 175 [3.11])

To explain this distinction, Pictet uses an illustration that has a dis-
turbing ring of truth:

> If anyone cannot conceive how the affection of hatred can be excited,
> without any direction to an object, let it be observed, that we are very
> often in such a state, as that all things displease us, and we are prepared
> to hate whatever objects may be presented to us, although there is no
> object particularly before us at the time.
>
> (175 [3.11])

This distinction between the material and the moral cause of an
action is perhaps the point at which the Reformed doctrine of
providence needs to be read most carefully. The purpose of the
distinction is obviously to explain how no act can occur apart from
divine concurrence with it, and yet how God is not the morally
culpable cause of any sin. The idea of material causation affirms
divine concurrence; the idea of moral causation denies divine cul-
pability. The difficulty is that the distinction might be taken to
suggest that there is a sphere of creaturely causation, the moral
sphere, in which the creature sins, but from which God is absent.
Pictet and Turretin cannot mean this given their insistence on total

divine concurrence in all human acts; the idea that something might exist in its own sphere is simply inadmissible.

It is when Pictet discusses the *progress* and *end* of sin that the significance of the material–moral distinction emerges most clearly. He explains that God directs the progress of sin by preventing it moving toward the end intended by the sinner. For example, God so overruled the actions of Joseph's brothers that they achieved the exaltation of Joseph, the opposite of what they intended (176–177 [3.11]). He says something similar about the end or goal of sin:

> The acts of divine Providence in regard to the *end* of sin, or sin when it *has been* committed, are various. One act is, the direction of the sin to a good end, as the selling of Joseph to the preservation of Jacob's family, and the crucifixion of Jesus Christ to the redemption of mankind.
>
> (177 [3.11])

This description of the way God relates to the progress and end of sin clarifies the point of the material–moral distinction: God is not morally related to sin in the way the sinner is. For the sinner, the act is one thing because it has a certain direction and goal. For God, it is another. In that sense, he is not the moral cause of the act when it is regarded as a sin, since it is defined as a sin because of its progress and end. This point is vital. The death of a man is neither good nor bad; its moral status depends on its context and on the purposes of its agents. The death of a man who dies in a fire trying to rescue a child is a good thing for him because of his good purpose, but for those who set fire to the house it is an evil.

Having laid out some of Pictet's doctrine of divine providence, we may now apply it to our understanding of the cross to see how it helps in distinguishing the action of God from the action of Pilate. First, the assertion of exhaustive providence closes off Weaver's approach. Here Pictet is at one with the biblical testimony: we cannot exclude God from the action of the cross, for it is his will and his plan.

Then we can apply Pictet's five points about the beginning of sin to the murderous actions of the Sanhedrin and Pilate. God wills the cross, but does not approve of their sin. God hands them

over to their sin, removing restraints that would have kept them
from it. God confronts them with a good object, Jesus himself, to
whom they react in sin. God allows Satan to assault Judas. God
stirs up thoughts in the opponents of Jesus that are in themselves
good, such as the thought that Jesus claimed to be the Son of
God, but which they turn to evil.

Lastly we can apply the material–moral distinction and Pictet's
account of the progress and end of sin. God is the author of the
action of the persecutors of Jesus, considered as real action, but
not considered with respect to its moral character as determined
by their intended outcome. Indeed in the suffering of Jesus itself
God intends not his death regarded as such, which the Jews
intended, but his saving work. Then he prevents the evil intentions
of the Jews from achieving their ends by raising Jesus from the
dead. God is not the author of their sin since he moves the persecutors as active material agents, but with different moral ends. On
this basis we can see how the death of Jesus measured by the
intention of the Father can be the highest good, but, measured by
the intention of the Jews, the greatest evil.

Thus the morality of the action of God in the suffering of Jesus
is wholly distinct from the immorality of the action of Satan,
Judas, the Sanhedrin, Herod and Pilate. They all act in the same
event, but their actions are so different that they are beyond moral
comparison. The Reformed doctrine of providence does not
remove all the mysteries of divine–human action, but it does show
us how to articulate a metaphysical framework, a theology of
action, that highlights the difference. It allows us to do justice to
the biblical testimony that God intended the cross, while affirming
that his action is distinct from, and does not validate, the evil
human actions described in the Gospels.

Attempts to deny retribution in the biblical texts

It remains the case, however, that God the Father and the Lord
Jesus Christ intended the cross to pay the retributive punishment
deserved by sinners. Although the Reformed doctrine of providence distinguishes the action of God from that of Pilate, it does
not diminish the affirmation that the Son bore the retributive punishment that his people deserved. God's action in the atonement

does not mandate violence, but it does entail accepting that God exacts the just retributive penalty for sin. Commenting on various attempts to make penal substitutionary atonement more palatable, Weaver rightly notes that this element is unavoidable: 'Satisfaction atonement *in any form* depends on divinely sanctioned violence that follows from the assumption that doing justice means to punish' (Weaver 2001: 203). For the reasons given above I would question the language of 'divinely sanctioned violence', but penal substitutionary atonement does depend on the idea that justice entails, among other things, retributive punishment. There is quite simply nothing that can be done to make this less offensive.

Where theologians such as Weaver have a problem with retribution, they have an intractable problem with the Bible itself, which ought to be a serious concern for theologians professing to be evangelical. For Scripture again and again depicts God exacting retributive punishment. Attempts at cherry-picking exegesis that expunge or minimize the retributive content of Scripture are doomed to failure. Weaver engages briefly with the biblical material, reviewing some of the biblical data and offering non-retributive readings of, for example, the work of the conquering Christ in Revelation. He points out that Christ conquers non-violently by the sword in his mouth, namely his word (2001: 20–33; the discussion of 19:11–21 is on p. 33). But such specifics are hardly sufficient when the Bible is replete with examples of divine retribution, such as the flood (Gen. 6 – 8), the destruction of Sodom and Gomorrah (Gen. 18 – 19), the Passover (Exod. 12), the drowning of the Egyptian army (Exod. 14), the deaths of Korah, Dathan and Abiram (Num. 16) and the attack on the Midianites (Num. 31) – to restrict ourselves to just some of the examples found in only the first four books of the Bible.

Stephen Travis against retribution

Some have engaged in more comprehensive attempts to reduce the retributive material in the Bible. Stephen Travis, for example, maintains that 'the judgment of God is to be seen not primarily in terms of retribution, whereby people are "paid back" according to their deeds, but in terms of relationship or non-relationship to

Christ' (Travis 1986: preface). Travis's case rests on the claim that retributive punishment has five characteristics:

1. What is inflicted is an *ill* – something unpleasant.
2. It is a *sequel* to some act which has gone before and is disapproved by authority.
3. There is some *correspondence* between the punishment and the deed which has evoked it.
4. The punishment is *inflicted from outside*, by someone's voluntary act.
5. The punishment is inflicted on the *criminal*, in virtue of his offence.

(1986: 3, summarizing Moberly 1968: 35–36)

Furthermore, Travis thinks that retribution cannot be personal, since it is focused on the punishment of an 'act' or 'deed':

> We may pose the question whether there is any real place for retribution (in the sense defined above) in the context of personal relationships. People are rewarded or punished not because of their character, but because of some specific overt act which they have done. Retribution thus operates on a less than fully personal level, and it deals with externals.

(5)

With this kind of definition it is no wonder that Travis finds a lack of retribution in the Bible. The definition is flawed in several ways; I will address only one of them here.[19] On the basis that retributive punishment must be '*inflicted from outside*, by someone's voluntary act', Travis argues that any negative consequences arising as a natural result of an act cannot be retributive. This is of course true in the case of retribution imposed by human beings, but it is not true in the case of divine retribution. The natural consequences of an act cannot be *human* retributive responses, but they may be *God's* retributive responses, for God controls the natural order within

---

19. For a discussion of further flaws, see G. J. Williams 2007: 73–76.

which those consequences occur. W. H. Moberly, on whose work Travis builds his definition, recognizes this explicitly: 'Disagreeable consequences which follow wrongdoing by natural causation, as disease or poverty sometimes follow, are not "punishment" unless they are supposed to be deliberately brought about by some super-human personal agency' (Moberly 1968: 35–36).

Travis, on the other hand, fails to make this distinction. This is deeply problematic for his entire project, for he relies on this aspect of the definition of retribution to deny the retributive character of many punishments described in Scripture. For example, he writes that 'the Jesus of the synoptic gospels sometimes uses retributive words, and some of these judgment-sayings are expressed in talionic *form*. But the *content* of such sayings generally undermines a strictly retributive interpretation' (Travis 1986: 134). How so? Because, we learn in Travis's discussion of the passage about treasure in heaven, 'Jesus pictures people's destinies as the end-result of their desires rather than as a recompense imposed from outside' (134). But according to the more careful definition offered by Moberly, this kind of punishment may still be retributive if the connection is established by God. Travis's attempt to expunge divine retribution from Scripture must be pronounced a failure.

Timothy Gorringe against retribution
Timothy Gorringe is another contemporary theologian who finds the idea of divine retribution abhorrent. Gorringe is deeply unhappy about how the idea of divine retribution has influenced penal systems during the history of the church. Although he recognizes the difficulty of establishing causal relations between theological views and cultural practices, he holds that 'the mutual reaction of penal theory and atonement theology led to a rhetoric of violence and the creation of a structure of affect where violence was legitimated' (Gorringe 1996: 24).

This allegation is similar to those we have seen already, but Gorringe handles the biblical data very differently. Whereas writers like Travis seek to reinterpret Scripture, Gorringe frankly recognizes that it contains an ineradicable retributive element. Instead of attempting to minimize it, he argues that the Bible contains two competing strands, a testimony and a counter-testimony, one emphasizing obedience, the other retribution and sacrifice. Gorringe identifies 'a thin but clear tradition which speaks of the "sacrifice" of obedience', dating back to what he thinks is the primitive stratum of biblical material (51). This strand is evidenced in texts such as Hosea 6:6:

> I desire steadfast love and not sacrifice,
>   the knowledge of God rather than burnt offerings.

Here we find not an explicit repudiation of sacrifice, but an emphasis on the lifestyle of obedience and thanksgiving that was actually required. As time passed, 'such an understanding sat uneasily alongside the tradition of expiatory, or propitiatory, sacrifice which gained such prominence after the exile' (53). The non-sacrificial world view of Jesus placed the emphasis clearly on the primitive element once again. Thus in the Gospels Jesus is twice recorded as quoting from Hosea 6:6 (Matt. 9:13; 12:7), and in the cleansing of the temple we find 'an implicit rejection of sacrifice' rather than just 'a desire for a stricter sacrificial cultus' (61).

Gorringe does not believe that we are simply caught between two incompatible strands of data: 'Are we left, then, with irreconcilable interpretations, equally justified in terms of appeal to the founding texts? I believe not. Our fundamental hermeneutic principle must be derived from the overall *direction* of the New Testament documents' (82). Gorringe is not here saying that the two strands cohere as part of the self-consistent word of God. Rather his claim is that one strand unmistakeably posits a dangerous view of retribution and sacrifice, and that this is finally displaced by another strand that has no place for it.

This approach is obviously unacceptable to anyone who thinks that taking the teaching of Jesus as authoritative means taking every word of the Bible as authoritative. If the word of God is not repugnant to itself, then we cannot speak in this way of competing, contradictory theological 'strands'. Of course, it is true that some portions of Scripture record sinful sentiments from the lips of human beings (some of Qoheleth's more gloomy moments spring to mind), or even the words of the devil himself. It is also true that different texts in Scripture contain different emphases, and that historical revelation is progressive. But none of these observations amounts to Gorringe's claim that so much of the teaching ascribed to God in Scripture (such as the Law given at Sinai, and many exilic and post-exilic texts) embodies a theology of sacrifice that must simply be rejected.

Indeed Gorringe rushes to posit incompatibility where a more careful reading would find synthesis. Consider for example the alleged contradiction between the biblical critique of hypocritical sacrifice and the sacrificial understanding of the death of Jesus. In passages like Hosea 6:6 we find not a rejection of sacrifice, but a demand that meaningful sacrifice requires moral transformation. Again, though Gorringe is surely right that Jesus' cleansing of the temple was a sign of coming judgment and rejection, this does not imply a wholesale rejection of the propitiatory sacrificial ideas that the temple embodied. The temple fell because of the final sacrifice made by Jesus and because of his rejection by the rulers of Jerusalem, not because God had changed his mind since the giving of the cultic laws. Gorringe's insistence that we find here two alternative strands of religion flows from a crude and literalistic reading of the text.

Despite these critical comments, my main purpose in citing the work of Gorringe is to show that he is in one sense a more accurate interpreter of the Bible than some of the Anabaptist critics of penal substitutionary atonement. Gorringe is more inclined to recognize that the Bible contains extensive retributive material than to reinterpret it by cherry-picking or legerdemain. It is less his interpretation and more his estimation of much of the biblical data that is problematic. Granting the presence of retribution, he is forced to posit a trajectory that undercuts much of the Bible's own description of God's work in the world. In effect, therefore, he grants that retribution cannot be rejected without setting aside a weighty strand of biblical evidence.

Such an approach will not, of course, be acceptable to those who hold that the words of the Bible are the words of God, a view that was held by Jesus himself, as John Wenham argues from the data of the Gospels: 'To Christ the Old Testament was true, authoritative, inspired. To him the God of the Old Testament was the living God

and the teaching of the Old Testament was the teaching of the living
God. To him, what Scripture said, God said' (Wenham 1993: 17).

Ethical implications of penal substitutionary atonement
I have argued that penal substitution is not unethical because God
is not violent in the same sense as Pilate. We now consider what
positive ethical lessons for the public square might be drawn from
the doctrine. On the basis of penal substitutionary atonement,
what might a contemporary Nathan say to his David, a prophet to
his king, the church to the state?

The legitimation of retribution
A perennial debate surrounds the idea that the state should impose
retributive punishment upon criminals. The argument of those
who oppose retribution is often that punishment should seek to
reform the offender, to protect society, and to deter potential criminals. The idea that it is good to punish a criminal for retributive
purposes, simply because he deserves it, is rejected. Yet it has been
successfully established among ethicists and philosophers of law
that the idea of retribution is necessary in order to secure the
justice of punishment. The other motives for punishment may be
laudable as additional aims, but without retribution they would
entail grievous miscarriages of justice. The retributive principle,
far from being an unethical and embarrassing monstrosity to be
eschewed by any just society, is an absolute necessity. As C. S.
Lewis famously argued, only the doctrine of retributive justice prevents the punishment of the innocent:

> The punishment of an innocent, that is, an undeserving, man is wicked
> only if we grant the traditional view that righteous punishment means
> deserved punishment. Once we have abandoned that criterion, all
> punishments have to be justified, if at all, on other grounds that have
> nothing to do with desert. Where the punishment of an innocent can be
> justified on those grounds (and it could in some cases be justified as a
> deterrent) it will be no less moral than any other punishment. Any
> distaste for it on the part of a Humanitarian will be merely a hang-over
> from the retributive theory.
>
> (Lewis 1970: 291–292)

Lewis provides a practical argument for the necessity of the retributive principle in punishment: without it, the innocent may be punished if it serves a useful purpose. By highlighting the dangers of abandoning the retributive principle, he shows why it is expedient to maintain it.

This is a powerful argument, but on its own it does not suffice to ground the retributive principle. If a society is to hold a properly grounded justification of what its rulers do when they punish, then it will need also to provide a firm theoretical basis for the inherent rightness of retribution. Otherwise, we have a retributive principle that defends the innocent, but it cannot tell us why they do not deserve punishment or why the guilty do. It is often very difficult for contemporary proponents of the retributive principle to find successful grounds for it because they disavow any appeals to metaphysics. But if we refuse to examine retribution within the context of the creature's relation to the Creator, then we will find that it has no basis within the reality of the universe. Ultimately it will be only a way of avoiding something we arbitrarily consider to be 'bad'.

At this point, the penal substitutionary doctrine of the atonement points toward how we may begin to construct a metaphysical justification for the rightness of retribution that goes beyond pointing out the dangerous legal and moral consequences of the alternatives. The doctrine teaches that God punishes sin retributively because he is holy. It appeals, in other words, to the being of God for the grounds of retribution. John Owen's *Dissertation on Divine Justice* is rich with material relevant to this theme. For example, Owen explores the necessity of what he terms 'vindicatory justice' by examining the biblical depiction of God as a consuming fire: 'As, then, consuming fire cannot but burn and consume stubble, when applied to it, so neither can God do otherwise than punish sin, that abominable thing, which is consuming or destroying it, whenever presented before him and his justice' (Owen 1967b: 553 [1.6]). But as he explains, God is no uncontrolled fire: 'He, indeed, is a fire, but rational and intelligent fire,' who chooses when and where he burns (603 [2.16]). Owen also argues that the necessity of retribution arises from the very structure of the relationship between man and God, a structure that cannot be altered because it is a feature of reality. He writes of 'the indispensable subordination of the creature to God; which, supposing disobedience or sin, could not otherwise be secured than by punishment' (511 [1.2]). Space prohibits developing these points further, but they begin to show how it is in considering the holy being of the Triune God, and our relation to him as creatures, that I will find the metaphysical ground for sin deserving punishment. Nathan will point out to David that there are proper metaphysical grounds for the justice-preserving retributive principle.

Penal substitutionary atonement also reminds us that the ruling authorities have a remit to punish retributively. We recall from our earlier discussion of Calvin, Olevianus and the Heidelberg Catechism that, according to the Reformed doctrine, God's retributive punishment was imposed on Christ through the instrumentality of the historic retributive acts of Pilate. The authority of Pilate to impose such a legal sentence is an indispensable element of the Reformed doctrine, for Christ was, as Olevianus observed, 'sentenced and condemned to death by God Himself through Pilate the judge' (Olevianus 1995: 65). Jesus states that authority was given to Pilate 'from above' (John 19:11); like all civil rulers he was one of the 'governing authorities (*exousiais hyperexousiais*)' who wielded the power of the sword to execute the wrath of God on the wrongdoer (Rom. 13:1–4).

This does not mean that penal substitution legitimates every individual sentence passed by a civil ruler. Pilate misused his power to execute an innocent man, and therefore stands condemned (Acts 4:24–27). As Olevianus put it, God was 'the one who pronounced the judgment through the mouth of Pilate', but Pilate 'had something quite different in mind' (65). Nevertheless, the doctrine does entail that civil rulers have authority to exact retribution. Again, it provides grounds for what might otherwise be little more than an assertion of the authority to punish made by the powerful. Nathan will remind his king that the authority and responsibility to punish has indeed been conferred on him.

The limitation of retribution
Retribution is prohibited for individuals by the teaching of Jesus (e.g. Matt. 5:38–42) and Paul (Rom. 12:14–21). It is prohibited to

individuals on the basis that it is the unique prerogative of God, as Paul explains in Romans 12:19: 'Beloved, never avenge yourselves, but leave it to the wrath of God, for it is written, "Vengeance is mine, I will repay, says the Lord."' According to the penal doctrine of the atonement, God not only will repay; he has already repaid, for he has taken retribution upon himself in Christ on the cross. The doctrine therefore bolsters the Pauline argument against people themselves seeking repayment for sin.

Penal substitutionary atonement with its co-requisite doctrines also shows why retribution is limited for the state. First, as Grotius reminds us, God is the ruler and the rule of humans is constrained under him. God himself defines and fills the space called 'ruler', leaving no space for others unless he delegates a measure of rule to them. We learn human concepts and apply them to God in obedience to their use in the Word of God. That is the order epistemologically. But ontologically it is the other way round: God defines the concepts; he gives them content. He is the true ruler, and earthly rulers are just pale imitations of his rule. If God were not construed as the supreme ruler, then the space called 'ruler' would indeed be vacant at a cosmic level, inviting anyone to define it and any tyrant to occupy it. But the space is filled. David will thus be cautioned by Nathan with the sober warning that he occupies a space owned by God at the pleasure of God. Authority to rule (and so to punish) *has* been conferred on him, but it has been *conferred* on him: it is not ultimately his.

Second, the ruler does not have freedom to punish just as he wishes, because God's own activity in punishment is defined by his holy nature. God is not pure will; he is holy will. Hence he himself, though he can do whatever he wills to do, will not will to do a whole range of things, including anything unjust. Penal substitution affirms the necessary justice of God's actions. Because God's own punishments are holy and perfect, a right to punish derived from him could only ever be a right to punish justly. Nathan will thus warn David that even God himself does not have an absolute carte blanche for any judicial action we with our sinful minds may conceive.

Third, the nature of our speech about God precludes us thinking that everything true of him is true also of a human ruler.

A connection is indeed drawn between God's rule and the ruler, but the connection is not, as we have seen, univocal. All that is true of God is not true of the ruler. There is therefore, written into the structure of the way we speak about God, a pervasive restraint on any claim that identifies the ruler with God, even given the restricted right to execute wrath on the wrongdoer that the ruler has. Nathan will thus remind David that just because he is a ruler, he cannot presume his own univocal identity with God.

Denial of extended or substitutionary punishment to rulers

Having described general grounds for the limitation of retribution by earthly rulers, it is possible to give a specific example. In the second commandment it is clear that God does enact transgenerational punishment among those who continue in the idolatry of their fathers: 'I the LORD your God am a jealous God, visiting the iniquity of the fathers on the children to the third and fourth generation of those who hate me, but showing steadfast love to thousands of those who love me and keep my commandments' (Deut. 5:9).

In Deuteronomy 24:16, however, we read this: 'Fathers shall not be put to death because of their children, nor shall children be put to death because of their fathers. Each one shall be put to death for his own sin.' There is no contradiction between these two passages: in the first God warns that he himself will punish transgenerationally, while in the second he prohibits rulers punishing citizens in the same way. God is not bound by the laws he sets for men, and men are not free with the freedom he himself exercises. This interpretation is supported by the other references to human conduct in Israelite society in the context of chapter 24. Here is a good example of the conflicting analogy between divine and human rule. If anyone attempts to argue that a ruler may punish transgenerationally by virtue of the right given in Romans 13, we find in the law of Israel a clear indication to the contrary. Thus a ruler may not extend punishment from one individual to another, and Pilate had no ground for punishing the innocent Jesus. In condemning Jesus despite recognizing his innocence, Pilate engaged in unjustified violence against him.

A question about divine consistency arises at this point. How is the punishment of the righteous Christ unjust for Pilate but acceptable as an act of God in Christ? How does the action of God not legitimate the action of Pilate? It is the framework of providence that helps us to see how the crucifixion could be a different act for God from what it was for Pilate. For God, while Jesus was wholly personally innocent, he was not innocent *simpliciter*; he was imputatively guilty. This imputation was just because the union between Jesus and his people was real and true. As Turretin explains, 'God willed to unite us to Christ by a twofold bond – one natural, the other mystical – in virtue of which both our evils might be transferred to Christ and the blessings of Christ pass over to us and become ours' (Turretin 1992–7, 2: 647 [16.3.5]).[20] The union was no pretence: 'we do not invent an imputation consisting in a mere opinion and fiction of law; but one which is in the highest sense real and true' (656 [16.3.30]). Hence within the realm of divine action Jesus was imputatively guilty and so justly bore substitutionary punishment. God did not punish an innocent man; he punished a personally innocent man. But that same man was imputatively guilty by union with his people. By contrast, for Pilate, Jesus was a wholly innocent man who had not committed the crimes of which he was accused. Pilate had no notion of the death of Jesus being a just substitution, nor did he have any authority to make it so. To think that substitutionary atonement mandates the infliction of suffering on the innocent is to miss this vital difference between God and Pilate. A ruler cannot find in the doctrine any basis for the unjust punishment of the innocent. Nathan must therefore forbid substitutionary punishment to David, showing him how Jesus bore imputed guilt on the basis of a constituted identity that no merely human king could ever establish.

Christians cannot be punished retributively
The doctrine of penal substitutionary atonement requires that we rethink what it means for a Christian to be punished by the state. The issue can be set out simply: if a Christian's eschatological

---

20. This is the section on the imputation of righteousness, but Turretin has an eye on the imputation of sin as well.

punishment has been exhaustively borne by Jesus, and if the state exercises in the present a foretaste of the wrath to come, then there is no wrath for the state to exercise against a Christian who has committed a crime, since Christ has already borne it. Key here is the way in which Paul's reference to the wrath administered by the authorities in Romans 13:4 follows and presumes the identification of this wrath with the future wrath of God in 12:19: the state enacts in the present a foretaste of the future wrath (noting the tense of *egō antapodōsō*). The fact that Jesus has borne the punishment for his people introduces a difficulty into the reading of Romans 13 itself, since it seems to indicate that the punishment of a Christian cannot conform to the description given here by Paul.

The puzzle of the punishment of those already punished in Christ is not explicitly addressed anywhere in Scripture. Perhaps the best way to understand it is to take Romans 13 as a general statement about the authorities and punishment, but to infer from what the rest of Scripture teaches about penal substitution that the punishment of Christians must be understood differently from the way Paul describes punishment in general at this point. Thinking that there is something unusual or exceptional about the punishment of Christians fits well with Paul's argument in the chapter: if there are Christians who commit crimes, they are indeed anomalous, since the governing authority ought to be no threat to the good, among whom Christ's people ought to be numbered. Christians ought not to need to be punished: something abnormal is going on if they do. Of course, if the ruler criminalizes what should not be criminalized, then Christians are wrongly punished and the ruler himself creates the anomaly.

The proper punishment of a Christian differs in its nature from the punishment of a non-Christian because it is not the present application of coming eschatological wrath. This difference is not, however, relevant to the conduct of the ruler, since the punishment is still to be imposed only on the guilty, is to be imposed in right proportion and is to have its usual purpose, to foster the good of the people (Rom. 13:4). The different character of the punishment matters for the Christian criminal rather than for the ruler, since for the Christian the punishment takes the form not of retribution but of discipline from the Lord's hand to one of his children whom he loves, much like parental discipline (Heb. 12:5–11). Above all, the different character matters to God, since in afflicting a Christian through the agency of the ruler he is imposing fatherly chastisement rather than retribution.

The ruler's punishment of Christians remains outwardly the same as the punishment of non-Christians for good reasons. First, the spiritual state of the criminal at the time of the punishment is unknown to the ruler, and it might change after the sentence has been passed, for example in the case of a prisoner converted while serving his sentence. The ruler is not competent to discern the difference between the believer and the unbeliever, since, unlike the church, the ruler does not hold the power of the keys to bind by means of excommunication.

Second, the punishment of Christians must retain echoes of retribution because it cannot safely be devoid of all the elements of retributive punishment. As we have seen, wholly non-retributive punishment would be arbitrarily imposed and thus unjust. Some notional element of desert must therefore be retained in the punishment of Christians to ensure that punishment is inflicted only on those who have committed crimes. Christ has borne the sins of his people, but there remains a difference between a Christian who has committed a crime and one who has not, even if it is not measured in terms of actual desert.

Third, the principle of proportionality that retribution requires must be upheld, since without it there would be no restraint on the severity of punishment. Christ has borne the sins of his people, but there remains a difference between a punishment that is notionally proportionate to a crime and one that is not, even if there is, *stricto sensu*, no desert to which the proportion of punishment responds.

Fourth, the ruler has the same outcome in mind when punishing the Christian and the non-Christian: a crime has been committed and it is his role to be a visible terror to those who do what is wrong (Rom. 13:3).

As an aside, it is worth noting that this argument from the atonement to the nature of the punishment of Christians has implications for our understanding of the extent of God's intention for the cross.

These implications can be highlighted by exploring an argument developed against the scapegoat theory of René Girard by William Placher. A brief account of the theory will allow us to introduce the objection.

Through a long series of evolving works, Girard claims that human societies are driven by people imitating others ('mimesis'), competing with them, and finally desiring violence against them. He thinks that societies throughout history have developed scapegoat mechanisms to vent the build-up of violence within their bounds. In such mechanisms, a scapegoat is identified and in an act of violence the harm arising from mimetic desire is poured out on him, so that for a while the community returns to more harmonious living. As Girard returned to Roman Catholicism, he argued that the gospel is the story of Jesus as the great scapegoat, but that the cross actually exposes and thereby undermines the scapegoat mechanism: 'Once the basic mechanism is revealed, the scapegoat mechanism, that expulsion of violence by violence, is rendered useless by the revelation' (cited in Placher 1999: 8).

It is at this point that Placher disagrees. While for Girard revelation is sufficient to transform, Placher thinks that the world will not be so easily changed: 'Is it enough to say, "Oh, now I get it, and I won't do it any more," and go our way?' (9). Instead Placher argues that the cross is an act of retribution, and that it is as such, rather than just as revelation, that it invalidates all further acts of retribution:

> Girard says we must stop scapegoating the innocent, but then seems to claim that if only we see the truth, the problems of guilt will go away. The gospel, however, offers not just a revelation but a redeemer, whose love enables those who are guilty to know themselves to be forgiven. I think the message of the cross is more radical than Girard sees: it is not just that we should stop scapegoating the innocent, but that we should stop punishing the guilty.
>
> (15)

Placher's reasoning is clear and hard to resist: Jesus has borne the punishment for sin, therefore the punishment has been borne and no punishment remains. He writes, 'since Christ occupies the place of sin, the good news is that there is no place for sinners to go where they will be apart from God' (15).

If Jesus died bearing the punishment for the sins of every individual without exception, then this would indeed follow: a universal atonement would eliminate all instances of subsequent retributive punishment. The difficulty with such a claim is that it leaves no example of punishment to which the teaching of Paul in Romans 13 can be applied. Whereas I have argued that the punishment of Christians is an anomalous exception because Christ has died for his people, Placher's argument would eliminate any possibility of retributive punishment for anyone. This would leave Paul describing an empty set as if it were the norm. This difficulty is resolved if we posit an atonement intended for the elect specifically, since then the punishment of Christians is an exception to a rule that remains generally true, until the conversion of the nations renders the norm irrelevant.

A sign pointing to a higher act

Within history there are ongoing proleptic instances of the coming wrath of God. As Paul writes, 'the wrath of God is revealed from heaven against all ungodliness and unrighteousness of men, who by their unrighteousness suppress the truth' (Rom. 1:18). This is a present reality: divine providence provides temporal instances of the wrath of God that are a partial foretaste of the last day. The acts of the governing authorities also remind us of the wrath to come, as Paul explains in Romans 13:1–7.

Nonetheless, as signs of wrath, the acts of providence and the ruler are dwarfed by the death of Jesus on the cross, in two ways. First, simply in terms of magnitude. In the public agony of the Son of God we see the most horrific glimpse of the wrath to come. The extent of the humiliation of the only-begotten Son of the Father in his humanity reveals to those with eyes to see the depths of hell itself. Amazingly at the same time we see that the wrath of God is not yet his last word toward us. The cross reveals the wrath of God against sin, but in so doing it reveals his unsurpassed mercy and love, the way in which our sin can be forgiven. As we see the depths, so we see the height: it is in seeing the depths of the suffering endured by the Son of God that we see the height of his mercy.

This shows why penal substitution is not a doctrine that places law above love in God: if law were placed above love, then there would be no atonement, there would be only the punishments of hell. Giles Fraser is wrong, therefore, to maintain that 'there are two archetypal ways of understanding the theology of Easter: one is structured around the notion of retribution; the other around the notion of forgiveness' (Fraser 2005: 16). Penal substitutionary atonement refuses this choice and adheres both to retribution and to forgiveness, to forgiveness through substitutionary retribution.

The greatness of the cross affects the way in which we estimate and locate the role of retributive punishment by rulers as a sign of the wrath to come. As they reveal the wrath of God, the acts of the ruler are relativized by the higher revelatory act of God in the cross. Whether he knows it or not, the ruler points away from himself toward the greater act of God in Christ. Nathan will therefore counsel David that even his divinely mandated acts of judgment are signs that point to a greater sign.

Theological grounds for representation

The idea of representation is key to the doctrine of penal substitutionary atonement. Christ is our substitute because he is our representative head: as our head, the one to whom we are united, he can do something that counts for us, but that we do not do ourselves. On the cross he bears the punishment of our sins as our representative so that his death truly counts for us. But he bears it as our substitute too, because the fact that he bears it means that we never will. This substitutionary work is at the heart of the glory of the gospel: Jesus Christ, who can act for us as our representative, acts as our substitute when he bears the punishment for sin, so that we do not have to bear it ourselves. Penal substitutionary atonement maintains these twin ideas of representation and substitution.

Modern Western political systems depend on the idea of representation. In England, for example, we are represented locally, nationally, within Europe, at the United Nations, and in many other ways. As we seek a ground for the rightness of retribution, so we must seek some basis in God's reality for these patterns of representation. O'Donovan argues in his consideration of Christ

as representative that human government must be understood
in the light of God's government, which means that it must be
understood in the light of what has been accomplished in Christ:

> We cannot discuss the question of 'secular' government, the question
> from which Western political theology has too often been content to
> start, unless we approach it historically, from a Christology that has been
> displayed in narrative form as Gospel.

(O'Donovan 1996: 133)

Moreover, to say that the reality of representation is 'just there'
would be to miss the way in which reality itself is centred on the
Lord Jesus Christ as its ground and goal. Scripture explicitly
teaches that certain aspects of earthly reality find their basis in the
prior reality of God as Father and Son, and in his relation to his
people. Thus we know that human fatherhood is based on God's
fatherhood (Eph. 3:14–15), and that marriage is based on Christ's
relationship with the church (Eph. 5:22–33). Creation is not *before*
Christ in the plan of God: it is *for* him.

We presume at this point some kind of supralapsarianism, an
understanding of the decrees of God that places Christ the
redeemer before the decision to create the world, thus maintaining
his absolute centrality. If the world is in the end not about us but
about Christ, if he is the Creator, sustainer and end of all things
(Heb. 1:1–4), then we have reason to think that the realities of
creation in their very structures point us to Christ. So then for representation: the patterns of representation we see in creation are
grounded in Christ our representative. This is all the more apparent when we remember that political kings represent people: given
that the Lord Jesus is the King of kings, it is no surprise that he is
the one in whom all representation finds its ground.

Conclusion

Here and now, as I look out of my window, I see no queue of
Members of Parliament or High Court judges shuffling down
the drive of Oak Hill College, nor have many presbyters been

approached for their advice by the government or judiciary. In our context, the content of this chapter may seem distinctly utopian. The atonement may indeed have implications for the way rulers act, but no one seems to care. What, one may wonder, is the point of setting out some of those implications when it is hard to conceive of anyone with any kind of influence being interested in them?

The point is found in the fact that elsewhere things are different, and that everywhere things will be different. Were we in parts of Africa or South America, we might reasonably expect Christendom to come soon.[21] One day, it will even return to Europe and to Britain, for we are promised that

> the earth will be filled
> > with the knowledge of the glory of LORD,
> > as the waters cover the sea.
> (Hab. 2:14)

The nations will come streaming to Zion, and the word of the Lord will go forth (Isa. 2:1–4); they will be the heritage of the Messiah, and the ends of the earth will be his possession (Ps. 2:8). The king will rule from sea to sea, from the river to the ends of the earth (Ps. 72:8). The rock will grow into the mountain that fills the world (Dan. 2:35).[22] In that day, David will heed his Nathan.

© Garry J. Williams, 2008

---

21. On the present and future state of global Christianity, see Jenkins 2002.

22. For an explanation and defence of this eschatological vision, see Mathison 1999.

5. INESCAPABLY POLITICAL: SERMON PREACHED IN OAK HILL CHAPEL

David Field

George Herbert's Lord and ours

We consider this morning the lordship of Jesus.[1] Let us acknowledge that lordship as we pray: 'Lord Jesus we give you praise that you are the Lord of all, Jew and Greek, living and dead, the Lord of all. And we pray now that you would enable us, by your Spirit's work, to acknowledge, experience, demonstrate and live out your lordship. That will result in blessing for us and honour to you and so we seek it in your name. Amen.'

As we join George Herbert in confessing 'My Lord', so we consider this morning how that confession – that 'Jesus is Lord' – is inescapably political. George Herbert resented constraints on his

---

1. What follows is the text of a sermon preached in Oak Hill Chapel on 27 Feb. 2007, the second in a series of three sermons on how 'The Gospel Is Inescapably Political'. In the church calendar George Herbert is especially remembered on 27 Feb.

life, resolved to throw them off, was then addressed by God, and so came to recognize that God is Lord indeed. In his poem *The Collar* he wrote:

I struck the board, and cry'd, No more.
I will abroad.
What! shall I ever sigh and pine?
My lines and life are free; free as the rode,
Loose as the winde, as large as store.
Shall I be still in suit?
Have I no harvest but a thorn
To let me bloud, and not restore
What I have lost with cordiall fruit?
Sure there was wine
Before my sighs did drie it: there was corn
Before my tears did drown it.
Is the yeare onely lost to me?
Have I no bayes to crown it?
No flowers, no garlands gay? all blasted?
All wasted?
Not so, my heart: but there is fruit,
And thou hast hands.
Recover all thy sigh-blown age
On double pleasures: leave thy cold dispute
Of what is fit and not. Forsake thy cage,
Thy rope of sands,
Which pettie thoughts have made, and made to thee
Good cable, to enforce and draw,
And be thy law,
While thou didst wink and wouldst not see.
Away; take heed:
I will abroad.
Call in thy deaths head there: tie up thy fears.
He that forbears
To suit and serve his need
Deserves his load.
But as I rav'd, and grew more fierce and wilde
At every word,

> Me thoughts I heard one calling, *Childe*:
> And I reply'd, *My Lord.*

And when *we* reply, 'my Lord', then we have learned the ABC of the Christian faith. We cannot get more basic than 'Jesus is Lord'. This is our baptismal confession and this is our earliest and most essential creed.

On the day of Pentecost Peter declared that 'God has made him both Lord and Christ, this Jesus whom you crucified' (Acts 2:36).

Paul assured the Roman Christians (Rom. 10:9) that 'if you confess with your mouth that Jesus is Lord and believe in your heart that God raised him from the dead, you will be saved'.

He told the Corinthian Christians (1 Cor. 8:5–6) that 'indeed there are many "gods" and many "lords" – yet for us there is one God, the Father, from whom are all things and for whom we exist, and one Lord, Jesus Christ, through whom are all things and through whom we exist'. Later (12:3) he claimed that 'no one speaking in the Spirit of God ever says "Jesus is accursed!" and no one can say "Jesus is Lord" except in the Holy Spirit'. And in 2 Corinthians 4:5 he summarized his gospel: 'what we proclaim is not ourselves, but Jesus Christ as Lord'.

Then again, through Paul's words (Phil. 2:10), the Father's demand rang out that 'at the name of Jesus every knee should bow, in heaven and on earth and under the earth, and every tongue confess that Jesus Christ is Lord, to the glory of God the Father'.

No, the heart of the Christian gospel, the foundation of the Christian faith, the beginning of the Christian life, the essence of the Christian claim is clear: 'Jesus is Lord'.

'Jesus is Lord': heard in different ways

But granted that the sound 'Jesus is Lord' fills the New Testament proclamation, are we to hear it as a single note or as a chord? Given the different settings in which these same words were announced and heard, it must surely be the latter.

If you were a *first-century Jew*, then you knew that the name of God, *YHWH*, was represented by the word *kyrios* in your favourite Greek translation of the Hebrew Scriptures. So when you heard the announcement that 'Jesus is *kyrios*', one of the things you would think would be, 'Oh, so the Creator God, the covenant God, who is going to step in and defeat the enemies of God's people that are too strong for God's people themselves, who is going to restore the nation and live with his people and bless them, *that* Creator, covenant God – that's Jesus then, is it?'

If you *lived in Corinth*, then you may have received invitations from time to time (actually they were more demands than invitations) from the lord Serapis to attend his table or from the lord Osiris or from the lady or mistress Isis. So when you heard 'Jesus is Lord', one of the things that might have come to your mind was, 'Oh, so Jesus is the one into whose mysteries and knowledge and fullness I need to enter if I am to be a proper human being and enjoy blessing.'

If you were a *Roman citizen*, in Rome or Philippi or Thessalonica, then at the heart of Paul's letter to the Christians in your city was his emphasis upon the lordship of Jesus. And living in those cities, when you heard that 'Jesus is Lord', you could not but think, 'Oh, so how does that relate to Caesar being lord?'

The first few verses of Romans (1:1–7) are about Paul, a slave of the King-Messiah Jesus, who was appointed as an authorized representative and messenger of King-Messiah Jesus and was set apart to announce the good news of the new administration, the change of dynasty, that came from God and that God had promised ages before. God had said that this change of dynasty, this new regime would be focused upon a person who would be a rightful heir to the throne, who would be a son of God, and who would start the world afresh. And, living in Rome, you would think, 'Yes, yes, I know that sort of thing, I've heard that before. You're talking about Augustus aren't you?'

But then Paul went on, '*Jesus Christ* our Lord. *He's* the one through whom we've been given this responsibility and this authority to bring all the nations into faithful obedience, the obedience of faith, loyalty, allegiance-that-makes-a-difference. All nations are to acknowledge that Jesus, King-Messiah, is Lord.'

'Jesus is Lord': a challenge to the powers

That's something of how you would have heard the first few verses of Paul's letter to you if you were a Christian in Rome. If you kept listening, then you wouldn't hear much about the 'Lord' until the mini-climax at the end of chapter 4 (to be taken up again in 10:8–13), faith 'will be counted to us who believe in him who raised from the dead Jesus our Lord, who was delivered up for our trespasses and raised for our justification' (vv. 24–25). Then you would hear in 5:1, 'Therefore, since we have been justified by faith, we have peace with God through our Lord Jesus Christ.' And there in Rome you would have heard about 'justice' and 'peace' and a 'lord' over and over again, throughout your life. You knew the name of the 'Lord' who brings justice and peace – it was Caesar, wasn't it? No. It's the Lord . . . Jesus. And you'd be hearing more of this Lord in chapter 10 and it would be a key theme in chapter 14 and so on. The *Lord* Jesus. It's a challenge to Caesar. Paul was like a little schoolboy coming up on to the stage in the middle of the assembly with the whole school watching and giving the Head a shove and saying, 'Step aside and sit down, there's a new authority now.' The proclamation in first-century Rome that 'Jesus is Lord' was such a provocation.

Similarly with the first chapter of Philippians. In effect, Paul says, 'I don't much mind whether it's from the mouths of keen Christian preachers or from the mouths of enemies of mine recounting my message out of envy and rivalry in order to make trouble. I don't care. So long as the words get out, "King-Messiah Jesus . . . Jesus is Lord"; that's all I want: that'll make me happy.'

And just as a Roman Christian reading Romans 10:12 ('the same Lord is Lord of all') 'knows' that this must be about Caesar, so a Christian in the Roman colony of Philippi reading what we know as the second chapter of Philippians will surely think, 'This is Caesar, isn't it?' But it's not. No, in Philippians 2, the *Lord* is Jesus.

Perhaps we go back to the very beginning of the New Testament. There in Matthew 2 Herod realized something was afoot, didn't he?

Or we go forward to everybody's favourite early church story – the martyrdom of Polycarp. We watch the constable Herod and

Nicetes, his father, who 'shifted Polycarp into their carriage and tried to persuade him as they sat by his side, urging, "Why? What harm is there in saying, 'Caesar is Lord' and sacrificing and the rest of it and so saving yourself?"' (Stevenson 1983: 20). We know the climax that's coming later on: 'the proconsul continued insisting and saying, "Swear and I release you. Curse Christ."' And we know Polycarp's reply, the Luther moment, which sends shivers down your spine: 'Eighty-six years have I served Him and He has done me no wrong. How then can I blaspheme my King who has saved me?' (21).

We go back to Herod, and the arrival of Jesus is a challenge to the powers. We move forward to Polycarp and loyalty to Jesus is a challenge to the powers. We look around the book of Revelation and find that there is a 'faithful witness' in 1:5, somebody who like Antipas (2:13) has been killed by the powers but that *this* faithful witness is the 'firstborn from among the dead' and, another challenge to the powers, is also the 'ruler of kings on earth' (Rev. 1:5). And he will be called 'King of kings and Lord of lords' (Rev. 19:16).

We take a look at the New Testament's two favourite psalms and we hear:

> The LORD says to my Lord:
>   'Sit at my right hand,
> until I make your enemies your footstool.'
> (Ps. 110:1)

And we read that,

> 'As for me, I have set my King
>   on Zion, my holy hill.'

> I will tell of the decree:
> The LORD said to me, 'You are my Son;
>   today I have begotten you.
> Ask of me, and I will make the nations your heritage,
>   and the ends of the earth your possession.
> You shall break them with a rod of iron
>   and dash them in pieces like a potter's vessel.'

> Now therefore, O kings, be wise;
>> be warned, O rulers of the earth.
> Serve the LORD with fear,
>> and rejoice with trembling.
> Kiss the Son,
>> lest he be angry . . .
> (Ps. 2:6–12)

Whether we go to Romans or Thessalonians or Philippians, to Herod or Polycarp or Revelation, or to the favourite psalms of the New Testament, we find that the arrival and exaltation of Jesus is a challenge to the powers, a challenge to Caesar.

Political maxims and preliminary political applications

And this challenge could be summarized in some political maxims:

1. Caesar acts as Saviour or Caesar acts as servant.
2. Caesar recognizes Jesus as Lord or rivals Jesus as Lord.
3. If Caesar rivals the gospel, then he is condemned; if he serves the gospel, then his subordinate authority is secured, legitimated, clarified, dignified and empowered.
4. The option before Caesar is not 'all or nothing', 'Lord or loser'. The option is 'false all or true something', 'false claim to absolute authority or true claim to subordinate authority'.
5. The gospel is not rubbishing Caesar; it is relativizing him.
6. To say that Caesar is not the Saviour is not to say that Caesar is nothing; it is to say that Caesar is a servant.

It's all there in *The Return of the King*. When Isildur's heir arrives, what is Denethor, the Steward, going to do? That is the question: what does the Steward do when the real king arrives? And there are only two possibilities: he can serve the true King or he can rival the true King.

Let's make some preliminary applications to politics of the fact that 'Jesus is Lord'.

Obviously all politicians should be Christians because, after all, God has commanded all men everywhere to repent. So everybody is under a moral obligation to be a Christian. All politicians *should* be Christians. Every knee *will* bow, Romans 14, and therefore every knee *should* bow, Philippians 2. Jesus *is* Lord, isn't he? The real world is the one over which the Lord Jesus has all authority and in which he is to have first place in all things. If you deny that, then you're out of touch with reality. And who'd want to be governed by people out of touch with reality? What would it be like if you had mad people in control?

So all politicians should be Christians and all Christian politicians should do the following seven things.

Politicians should give explicit allegiance to Jesus and seek the same from others

Jesus is Lord everywhere, so it doesn't matter which hat you're wearing. It's not that when I'm in the church I wear my 'Jesus is Lord' hat and when I'm a father in my family I wear my 'Jesus is Lord' hat but, of course, when I'm being a politician I leave my hat on the stand. No, you wear your 'Jesus is Lord' hat everywhere. We are happy to write over the church doors that Jesus is Lord; we are happy to write over the front door of our house that Jesus is Lord. So why is it that some Christians, coming to the doors to the Houses of Parliament, say, 'Oh no, don't write anything over those doors'? For Jesus is Lord there, too.

Politicians, of all people, must acknowledge that there is no space over which Jesus is not Lord. There's no area of life over which he is not Lord. We must not say, 'Peaceful feelings deep in my chest-stomach area: Jesus is Lord. The best way of looking after my family: Jesus is Lord. The soundest and sanest ordering of the community, of a society of human beings . . . oh no, don't mention that Jesus is Lord.' There's no matter of public policy, no item to be dealt with in committee, no chapter in the party's manifesto that you can come to and say, 'The lordship of Jesus is not relevant here.' So politicians are to be explicit about that in their allegiance to his lordship.

You might think, 'But none of us sitting in chapel this morning are politicians.' Nevertheless, I hope that as future ministers we intend, Lord's Day by Lord's Day to be leading the congregations

committed to our charge in intercessions for those in authority. So
we'll want to know what to pray, won't we? And, in any case, you
may very well have people who are involved in politics in your con-
gregation – and you'll want to be a Bible teacher to them in their
calling as well as to others in their callings.

Don't be ashamed of the gospel

Don't be embarrassed about announcing that Jesus' empire has
arrived. You don't really want a change of government at the
highest level do you, because government at the top tier is the government of the Lord Jesus Christ: a change of government at that
level would be a disaster, if it weren't an absolute impossibility.

   You might want a change of government at the second tier but
remember that the key political reality, forming the environment in
which politicians operate, is fixed and sure. Every now and then the
commentators, the Andrew Marrs or Nick Robinsons, stand in
front of Number 10 and, because of significant political event X or
Y, declare, 'The rules of the game have now changed . . . we're in a
whole new territory.' Well, the environment in which you operate as
a politician, the rules of the game, are determined primarily not by
matters such as 'Tony Blair has announced that he is going to step
down in July' or 'the demographic time bomb' or 'climate change'
or 'the geopolitical monster of Islam' or other such things. The key
political reality is that Jesus is Lord. That sets the rules of the game:
Jesus is Lord. That's the air you breathe if you're a politician; and if
you fail to breathe it, you'll die. It's the space you occupy. Don't be
ashamed of it, then, as a Christian politician.

Be patient

Whose timescales are you working to as a politician? Usually politicians are some of the most frantic people on the planet, so driven
by what has happened in the last twenty-four hours and what might
happen in the next twenty-four hours. Well, Christian politicians,
that is, right-minded politicians, should think of political history as a
five-day match and of their whole political career as one minute of
that match. Your whole life is one minute in a five-day match. Think
beyond your lifetime. Think of the spread of the gospel, the building of the church, the discipling of the nations. Think of God's

purposes, God's promises and God's will. Have the sort of patience, the sort of relaxedness that comes from gospel confidence. After all, of the increase of *his* government and peace there will be no end. Relax a bit. Be patient.

Live as servants and with integrity

Because to relativize politics isn't to demean it but actually to dignify it. How so? Because when you relativize it, you say to politics, 'You're a servant,' and to politicians, 'You're servants.' But where does Jesus teach us that true greatness and dignity are to be found? In service. So when you relativize politics and politicians and tell them that they are at the service of King Jesus, you are not being disrespectful to them nor demeaning them but rather, you are dignifying them.

Which would you prefer to be? A self-proclaimed fool-king, issuing your orders and heading for judgment, or a legitimate steward-servant, honoured by the true King as and because you serve his people?

Make sure your means and your methods reflect the lordship of Jesus. If you're a Christian politician, don't look at the liars and the bribers and those who promise favours to interest groups and think, 'Oh, if only I were allowed to be dishonest as they are allowed to be dishonest, then I'd really begin to make some progress.' Don't resent them: they're killing themselves. Be glad that obedience to King Jesus liberates you to be *truly* effective.

Remember Judgment Day

There are massive temptations upon politicians and they need so very much to imagine Judgment Day and rehearse for it now. Mr Blair, Mr Brown, Mr Cameron and all the rest of them are going to be on their knees before the Lord Jesus Christ on that day. Practise now. Start rehearsing. Bring into the present the fact that you are a servant of the Lord Jesus, the King-Messiah. See yourself this way. See other politicians this way.

Obviously there's much to be said about professing Christians and church discipline and matters of that sort as an application of Judgment Day thinking in the present. But for the moment, just remember Judgment Day.

Pray and hope for the persecuted church

Jesus is Lord, *therefore* the persecuted church, and we along with these dear brothers and sisters, can pray for and be sure of vindication. Barnabas Fund supporters will not forget in a hurry 20 December 2006. There we were, hundreds and thousands of Barnabas Fund prayer supporters, scattered around the country and the world with our Barnabas Fund prayer news. The entry for that day ran, 'Pray that President Niyazov [of Turkmenistan] will realize that the Church cannot be squeezed out of existence and will cease his campaign against Christians.' So there we were at about quarter past seven that evening, 20 December, having our family prayers and one of my daughters prayed that President Niyazov would die one way or another. Best of all would be if he 'died' by being converted; if not that, then by being politically disempowered; and if not that, by ceasing to breathe. When, next morning, we switched on the news we heard that at about 8.30 the previous evening President Niyazov had died.

So we pray for our brothers and sisters who are being persecuted that the God of vengeance would rise up (Ps. 94). We pray that the arrows of King-Messiah Jesus would be sharp in the heart of his enemies and that the peoples would fall under him (Ps. 45). Yes, we'd love them to be sharp for conversion. But if we love our enemies and they're not going to get converted, then the sooner they die, the better for them anyway. We pray that the enemies of Jesus will lick the dust, preferably in voluntary submission (Ps. 72). And we pray for the persecuted church with confidence.

Intercede for rulers

So as we intercede for rulers and pray about rulers, week by week, we do so on the basis of the fact that Jesus is Lord. Not mealy-mouthed lowest-common-denominator prayers for vague 'humility and integrity' in the abstract. There *is* no authentic or lasting humility or integrity outside the Lord Jesus Christ, anyway. Pray, 'Father in heaven, the fact is that your Son, Jesus, is Lord, so please send your Holy Spirit and wake up these rebel politicians to that fact.' At our special services we say how wonderful it is to have our local MP or Mr Mayor or Mrs Mayor or Ms Mayor with us, and then we pray for them, 'Father, we thank you for these servants of yours.

Please help them to be wise and faithful servants by waking them up each and every morning to the realization and the glad confession that Jesus Christ is Lord. Help them to live, in every dimension of their lives, in the light of that fact. If they don't realize it yet, please make them realize it. If they do realize it, help them to live consistently with that realization.' Pray for those in authority in the light of the inescapably political fact that Jesus is Lord.

Jesus is Lord and applying that to politics is a bit of a strange thing for us. It's a bit like getting ready to play on a golf course for the first time, but at the moment we're not even allowed access to the course. So what will we do? Well, the best preparation is surely to play at our home course (and at the practice ground, I suppose) as well as we possibly can. We get into the groove so that when we go to the new course, even though we make a few mistakes because we misjudge where the bunker is or whether we can carry that dog-leg (a hole where the fairway has a bend) or suchlike, nevertheless at least our swing is smooth and we're striking the ball sweetly. That's not meant to sound like a Liberal Democrat conference speech – 'Go back to your constituencies and prepare for government' – no, it's not like that. It's to say that Jesus is Lord, we don't know exactly where we're going and nor do we know where his church is going over the next five minutes or five hundred years but we do know the ultimate destination and therefore the broad direction. We do know that we are meant to be getting in the groove of living with Jesus as Lord today.

That means that today we submit to the Scriptures in everything. That means that today we serve one another in our conversations. That means that today we live full of praise because he really is the Lord and full of hope because we know that all kings will fall down before him and all nations will serve him.

Let's pray together: 'We give you praise, Lord Jesus, that you are Lord. And we ask for your help for ourselves, for our persecuted Christian brothers and sisters, for Christian politicians, for politicians who don't recognize that you are Lord. Please deal with each of us just as we have need so that you are honoured just as you should be. We ask it in your name. Amen.'

BIBLIOGRAPHY

AQUINAS, T. (1924–9), *Summa contra gentiles*, trans. English Dominican Fathers (London: Burns, Oates & Washbourne).

— (1981), *Summa theologica*, trans. Fathers of the English Dominican Province, 5 vols. (Westminster: Christian Classics).

BACOTE, V. E. (2005), *The Spirit in Public Theology: Appropriating the Legacy of Abraham Kuyper* (Grand Rapids: Baker).

BARROW, S., and BARTLEY, J. (2005) (eds.), *Consuming Passion: Why the Killing of Jesus Really Matters* (London: Darton, Longman & Todd).

BARTH, K. (1956), *Church Dogmatics*, IV/1, ed. G. W. Bromiley and T. F. Torrance, trans. G. W. Bromiley (Edinburgh: T. & T. Clark).

BATES, S. (2007), *God's own Country: Tales from the Bible Belt: Power and the Religious Right in the USA* (London: Hodder & Stoughton).

BAVINCK, H. (1966), *Church Between Temple and Mosque* (Grand Rapids: Eerdmans).

BENNE, R. (1995), *The Paradoxical Vision: A Public Theology of the Twenty-first Century* (Augsburg: Fortress).

BIRKETT, K. (1997), *Unnatural Enemies: An Introduction to Science and Christianity* (Sydney: Matthias Media).

BOERSMA, H. (2004), *Violence, Hospitality, and the Cross: Reappropriating the Atonement Tradition* (Grand Rapids: Baker).

BOLT, J. (2001), *A Free Church, a Holy Nation: Abraham Kuyper's American Public Theology* (Grand Rapids: Eerdmans).

BOLT, P. (1998), 'Mission and Witness', in I. H. Marshall and D. Peterson (eds.), *Witness to the Gospel: The Theology of Acts* (Grand Rapids: Eerdmans), 191–214.

BROWN, H. O. J. (1989), 'The Christian America Major Response', in G. S. Smith (ed.), *God and Politics: Four Views on the Reformation of Civil Government* (Phillipsburg: P. & R.), 252–257.

BUDZISZEWSKI, J. (1997), *Written on the Heart: The Case for Natural Law* (Downers Grove: IVP).

CALVIN, J. (1667), *Catechismus ecclesiae Genevensis in tractatus theologici omnes* (Amsterdam: Ionnes Iacobus Schipper).

— (1834), *Institutio christianae religionis*, ed. A. Tholuck, 2 vols. (Berlin: Gustavus Eichler).

— (1954), *The Catechism of the Church of Geneva in Calvin: Theological Treatises*, trans. J. K. S. Reid (Philadelphia: Westminster).

— (1960), *Institutes of the Christian Religion*, ed. J. T. McNeill, trans. F. L. Battles, 2 vols. (Philadelphia: Westminster).

CARSON, D. A. (2008), *Christ and Culture Revisited* (Grand Rapids: Eerdmans; Nottingham: Apollos).

CHAPLIN, J. (2004), 'Defining "Public Justice"', in a Pluralistic Society: Probing a Neo-Calvinist Insight', *Pro rege* (Mar.): 1–11.

CHESTER, T. (1993), *Awakening to a World in Need: The Recovery of Evangelical Social Concern* (Leicester: IVP).

— (2002) (ed.), *Justice, Mercy and Humility: Integral Mission and the Poor* (Carlisle: Paternoster).

— (2004), *Good News to the Poor: Sharing the Gospel through Social Involvement* (Leicester: IVP).

CHESTER, T., and TIMMIS, S. (2007), *Total Church: A Radical Reshaping around Gospel and Community* (Leicester: IVP).

CLARK, S. (2005), *Tales of Two Cities* (Leicester: IVP).

COEKIN, R. (2006), 'The Priority of Gospel Ministry', in V. Roberts and T. Thornborough, *Workers for the Harvest Field* (New Malden: Good Book), 33–48.

COFFEY, J. (2004), 'The State and Social Transformation', in D. Hilborn (ed.), *Movement for Change: Evangelical Perspectives on Social Transformation* (Carlisle: Paternoster), 95–112.

— (1997), *Politics, Religion and the British Revolutions: The Mind of Samuel Rutherford* (Cambridge: Cambridge University Press).

COOK, C. (2004), *Pears Cyclopaedia*, 112th ed. (London: Penguin).

D'COSTA, G. (2004), 'On Theology's Babylonian Captivity', in J. Astley, L. Francis, J. Sullivan and A. Walker (eds.), *The Idea of a Christian University: Essays in Theology and Higher Education* (Milton Keynes: Paternoster), 183–199.

— (2005), *Theology in the Public Square: Church Academy and Nation* (Oxford: Blackwell).

DALE, R. W. (1899), *The Atonement* (London: Congregational Union of England and Wales).

EDERSHEIM, A. (1897), *The Life and Times of Jesus the Messiah*, 2 vols. (London: Longmans, Green).

ELLIOTT, M. (2005), 'Editorial', *European Journal of Theology* 14.

EUSEBIUS (1995 [1890–1900]), *The Life of Constantine*, Nicene and Post-Nicene Fathers, Series 2, American ed., vol. 1 (Buffalo: Christian Literature Publishing; repr. Peabody: Hendrickson).

EVANGELICAL ALLIANCE (2006), *Faith and Nation: Report of a Commission of Inquiry* (London: Evangelical Alliance).

EVANS, G. R. (1989), *Anselm* (London: Geoffrey Chapman).

FESKO, J. V. (2007), *Last Things First: Unlocking Genesis 1–3 with the Christ of Eschatology* (Fearn: Mentor).

FIELD, D. (2007), 'Not the Least Lash Lost' <http://davidpfield.com/other/AAPC2-3lecture.pdf> (accessed 2 Oct. 2007).

FINNIS, J. (1983), *Fundamentals of Ethics* (Georgetown: Georgetown University Press).

— (1991), *Moral Absolutes: Tradition, Revision and Truth* (Washington: Catholic University of America Press).

FRAME, J. (1995), *Cornelius Van Til: An Analysis of His Thought* (Phillipsburg: P. & R.).

— (2001), 'Christianity and Culture: Lecture 1 – What Is Culture?', Lectures given at the Pensacola Theological Institute, 23–27 July 2001 <http://www.thirdmill.org/newfiles/joh_frame/Frame.Apologetics2004.ChristandCulture.pdf> (accessed 2 Oct. 2007).

— (2007), 'Chapter 17: Our Chief Aim', in *Doctrine of the Christian Life* (unpublished) <http://reformedperspectives.org/newfiles/joh_frame/dcl17_our_chief_end.doc> (accessed 2 Oct. 2007).

FRASER, G. (2005), 'The Easter of Hawks, Doves, Victims and Victimisers', in Barrow and Bartley (2005: 12–18).

GAY, P. (1995 [1966]), *The Enlightenment; an Interpretation: The Rise of Modern Paganism* (New York: Knopf; repr. New York, Norton).

— (1977 [1969]), *The Enlightenment; an Interpretation: The Science of Freedom* (New York: Knopf; repr. New York, Norton).

GILLMAN, I. (1961), 'Constantine the Great in the Light of the Christus Victor Concept', *Journal of Religious History* 1: 197–205.

GOLDSWORTHY, G. (2000), 'Gospel', in T. D. Alexander and B. S. Rosner (eds.), *New Dictionary of Biblical Theology* (Downers Grove: IVP; Leicester: IVP), 521–524.

GORRINGE, T. (1996), *God's Just Vengeance: Crime, Violence and the Rhetoric of Salvation* (Cambridge: Cambridge University Press).

GRABHILL, S. J. (2006), *Rediscovering the Natural Law in Reformed Theological Ethics* (Cambridge: Eerdmans).

GROTIUS, H. (1990), *Defensio fidei catholicae de satisfactione Christi adversus Faustum Socinum Senensem*, in E. Rabbie (ed.) and H. Mulder (trans.), *Hugo Grotius opera theologica*, vol. 1 (Assen: Van Gorcum).

HART, D. (1999), 'What Can Presbyterians Learn from Lutherans?', *Logia* 8: 3–7.

— (2006), *A Secular Faith: Why Christianity Favors the Separation of Church and State* (Chicago: Ivan R. Dee).

HEGEMAN, D. B. (1999), *Plowing in Hope: Toward a Biblical Theology of Culture* (Moscow: Canon).

HENGEL, M. (1977), *Crucifixion*, trans. J. Bowden (London: SCM).

HILL, M. (2007), 'An Evangelical Rationale for Social Action' <http://www.matthiasmedia.com.au/briefing/webextra/socialaction.pdf> (accessed 2 Oct. 2007).

HIMMELFARB, G. (2004), *The Roads to Modernity: The British, French and American Enlightenments* (New York: Knopf).

HOEKEMA, A. (1979), *The Bible and the Future* (Carlisle: Paternoster).

HOLLOWAY, D. (2007), 'Fundamentalism and Islam' <http://www.church.org.uk/resources/csdetail.asp?csdate=01/08/2005> (accessed 2 Oct. 2007).

HUGHES, D. (2001), 'Why the Reformed Suspicion of Social Action?', *Evangel* 19.1: 24–28.

JENKINS, P. (2002), *The Next Christendom: The Coming of Global Christianity* (Oxford: Oxford University Press).

— (2006), *The New Faces of Christianity* (Oxford: Oxford University Press).

JOHNSTONE, R. K. (1979), *Evangelicals at an Impasse: Biblical Authority in Practice* (Louisville: Westminster John Knox).

JOSEPHUS, F. (1968), *The Jewish War*, trans. H. St. J. Thackeray, in *Josephus in Nine Volumes*, vol. 3, Loeb Classical Library 210 (London: Heinemann).

JUSTIN MARTYR (1995 [1885–96]), *First Apology*, Ante-Nicene Fathers, American ed., vol. 1 (Buffalo: Christian Literature Publishing; repr. Peabody: Hendrickson).

KELLER, T. (1989), *Ministries of Mercy: The Call of the Jericho Road* (Grand Rapids: Zondervan).

— (2007), 'The Centrality of the Gospel' <http://www.redeemer2.com/resources/papers/centrality.pdf> (accessed 2 Oct. 2007).

KIM, S. (2007), 'Editorial', *International Journal of Public Theology* 1.

KIPLING, R. (1990), *Gunga Din and Other Favorite Poems*, ed. S. Applebaum (Mineola: Dover).

KLINE, M. (1972), *The Structure of Biblical Authority* (Grand Rapids: Eerdmans).

KRAEMER, H. (1939), 'Continuity or Discontinuity', in W. Paton (ed.), *The Authority of Faith* (London: Oxford University Press), 1–21.

LEITHART, P. J. (1995), *Did Plato Read Moses? Middle Grace and Moral Consensus*, Biblical Horizons Occasional Paper 23 (Florida: Biblical Horizons).

— (1996), *Natural Law: A Reformed Critique*, Biblical Horizons Occasional Paper 25 (Niceville: Biblical Horizons).

— (1999), *Heroes of the City of Man: A Christian Guide to Select Ancient Literature* (Moscow: Canon).

— (2003), *Against Christianity* (Moscow: Canon).

— (2007), 'Mirror of Christendom' <http://www.marshillaudio.org/resources/pdf/Leithart.pdf> (accessed 2 Oct. 2007).

LEWIS, C. S. (1970), *God in the Dock: Essays on Theology and Ethics*, ed. W. Hooper (Grand Rapids: Eerdmans).

LINCOLN, A. T. (2000), *Truth on Trial: The Lawsuit Motif in the Fourth Gospel* (Peabody: Hendrickson).

MACHEN, J. G. (1923), *Christianity and Liberalism* (New York: Macmillan).

MARSDEN, G. (1996), *The Soul of the American University: From Protestant Establishment to Established Unbelief* (Oxford: Oxford University Press).

MARSHALL, C. D. (2003), 'Atonement, Violence and the Will of God: A Sympathetic Response to J. Denny Weaver's *The Nonviolent Atonement*', *Mennonite Quarterly Review* 77.1: 69–92.

MATHISON, K. A. (1999), *Postmillennialism: An Eschatology of Hope* (Phillipsburg: P. & R.).

MELITO OF SARDIS (1979), *On Pascha and Fragments*, ed. S. G. Hall (Oxford: Clarendon).

MOBERG, D. (1973), *The Great Reversal: Evangelism versus Social Concern* (London: Scripture Union).

MOBERLY, W. H. (1968), *The Ethics of Punishment* (London: Faber & Faber).

MOO, D. J. (1996), *The Epistle to the Romans* (Grand Rapids: Eerdmans).

MOUW, R. (2001), *He Shines in All That's Fair: Culture and Common Grace* (Cambridge: Eerdmans).

MURRAY, J. (1976), 'The Relation of Church and State', *Collected Writings of John Murray*, vol. 1 (Edinburgh: Banner of Truth), 253–259.

MURRAY, J. (1977), 'Common Grace', *Collected Writings of John Murray*, vol. 2 (Edinburgh: Banner of Truth, 1977), 93–122.

MURRAY, S. (2005), 'Rethinking Atonement after Christendom', in Barrow and Bartley (2005: 27–35).

MYERS, K. (1994), 'Natural Law without Shame', *Tabletalk* 18: 5.

NIEBUHR, H. R. (2001), *Christ and Culture*, rev. ed. (San Francisco: HarperCollins).

NIETZSCHE, F. W. (1968), *Twilight of the Idols*; and *The Anti-Christ*. Trans., with an introduction and commentary, R. J. Hollingdale (Baltimore: Penguin).

NOLL, M. A. (1991) (ed.), *Confessions and Catechisms of the Reformation* (Leicester: Apollos).

— (1994), *The Scandal of the Evangelical Mind* (Leicester: IVP).

NORTH, G. (1990), *Millennialism and Social Theory* (Tyler: Institute for Christian Economics).

NORTHCOTT, M. (2005), 'Atonement, Violence and Modern Imperial Order', in Barrow and Bartley (2005: 89–98).

O'BRIEN, P. T. (1982), *Colossians and Philemon* (Waco: Word).

O'DONOVAN, O. (1994 [1986]), *Resurrection and Moral Order: An Outline for Evangelical Ethics* (Leicester: Apollos; Grand Rapids: Eerdmans).

— (1996), *The Desire of the Nations: Rediscovering the Roots of Political Theology* (Cambridge: Cambridge University Press).

OLEVIANUS, C. (1995), *A Firm Foundation: An Aid to Interpreting the Heidelberg Catechism*, ed. and trans. L. D. Bierma (Grand Rapids: Baker).

OWEN, J. (1967a), *The Death of Death in the Death of Christ*, in W. H. Goold (ed.), *The Works of John Owen*, vol. 10 (Edinburgh: Banner of Truth).

— (1967b), *A Dissertation on Divine Justice*, in W. H. Goold (ed.), *The Works of John Owen*, vol. 10 (Edinburgh: Banner of Truth Trust).

PHILLIPS, M. (2006), *Londonistan* (New York: Encounter).

PICTET, B. (1834), *Christian Theology*, trans. F. Reyroux (London: Seeley & Burnside).

PLACHER, W. C. (1999), 'Christ Takes our Place: Rethinking Atonement', *Interpretation* 53.1: 5–20.

PLANTINGA, C., Jr. (1983), 'The Concern of the Church in the Socio-Political World: A Calvinist and Reformed Perspective', *Calvin Theological Journal* 28.2: 190–205.

PLUTARCH (1999), *Roman Lives: A Selection of Eight Roman Lives*, ed. P. A. Stadter, trans. R. Waterfield (Oxford: Oxford University Press).

PULLMAN, P. (1995), *Northern Lights* (London: Scholastic).

— (1997), *The Subtle Knife* (London: Scholastic).

— (2001), *The Amber Spyglass* (London: Scholastic).

PUTNAM, R. (2000), *Bowling Alone* (New York: Simon & Schuster).

ROBERTSON, A. T. (1919), *A Grammar of the Greek New Testament in the Light of Historical Research* (London: Hodder & Stoughton).

ROMANOWSKI, W. (1996), *Pop Culture Wars* (Downers Grove: IVP).

RUSHDOONY, R. J. (1973), *Institutes of Biblical Law* (Phillipsburg: P. & R.).

— (1986), *Christianity and the State* (Vallecito: Ross House).

RUTHERFORD, S. (1644), *Lex, rex* (London).

— (1649), *A Free Disputation against Pretended Liberty of Conscience* (London).

SAMPSON, A. (2004), *Who Runs This Place? An Anatomy of Britain in the 21st Century* (London: John Murray).

SCHLOSSBERG, H. (1990), *Idols for Destruction* (Wheaton: Crossway).

SCHLUTER, M., and ASHCROFT, J. (2005) (eds.), *Jubilee Manifesto: A Framework, Agenda and Strategy for Social Reform* (Leicester: IVP).

SELBOURNE, D. (2005), *The Losing Battle with Islam* (New York: Prometheus).

SIRE, J. W. (2004a), *Naming the Elephant: Worldview as a Concept* (Downers Grove: IVP).

— (2004b), *The Universe Next Door*, 4th ed. (Downers Grove: IVP).

SOOKHDEO, P. (2005), *Islam in Britain: The British Muslim Community in February 2005* (Pewsey: Isaac).

SPENCER, N. (2006), *Doing God: A Future for Faith in the Public Square* (London: Theos).

STEVENSON, J. (1983 [1957]) (ed.), 'The Martyrdom of Polycarp', in *A New Eusebius* (London: SPCK, repr.), 18–26.

STEYN, M. (2006), *America Alone* (Washington, D. C.: Regnery).

— (2007), 'Facing Down Iran' <http://www.city-journal.org/html/16_2_iran.html (accessed 8 Sept. 2007).

STIBBE, M. G. W. (1993), *John* (Sheffield: JSOT).

STORRAR, W. F., and MORTON, A. R. (2004) (eds.), *Public Theology for the 21st Century: Essays in Honour of Duncan B. Forrester* (London: T. & T. Clark).

THIESSEN, V. (2005), 'The Passion and God's Transforming Love', in Barrow and Bartley (2005: 36–46).

TINGLE, R. (1995), 'Evangelical Social Action Today: Road to Recovery or Road to Ruin?', in M. Tinker, (ed.), *The Anglican Evangelical Crisis* (Fearn: Christian Focus), 186–202.

TINKER, M. (2001), 'Reversal or Betrayal? Evangelicals and Socio-political Involvement in the Twentieth Century', in M. Tinker, *Evangelical Concerns:*

Rediscovering the Christian Mind on Issues Facing the Church Today (Fearn: Mentor), 139–166.

— (2007), 'The Servant Solution: The Co-ordination of Evangelism and Social Action', *Themelios* 32.2: 6–32.

TRACY, D. (1975), *Blessed Rage for Order: The New Pluralism in Theology* (New York: Seabury).

— (1981), 'Defending the Public Character of Theology', *Christian Century* (1 Apr.): 350–356.

TRAVIS, S. H. (1986), *Christ and the Judgment of God: Divine Retribution in the New Testament* (Basingstoke: Marshall Pickering).

TUIT, P. C. (2000), 'A Study and Comparison of the Relationship Between Church and Kingdom in the Missiologies of J. H. Bavinck and D. J. Bosch' (ThM diss., Westminster Theological Seminary).

— (2006), 'The Relationship Between the Great Commission and World Transformation: Outline for a Reformed Missiology', in A. C. Leder (ed.), *For God So Loved the World: Missiological Reflections in Honor of Roger S. Greenway* (Belleville, Ont.: Essence), 113–142.

TURRETIN, F. (1992–7), *Institutes of Elenctic Theology*, ed. J. T. Dennison, trans. G. M. Giger, 3 vols. (Phillipsburg: P. & R.).

TYRRELL, G. (1910), *Christianity at the Cross-Roads* (London: Longmans, Green).

VAN DRUNEN, D. (2006), *A Biblical Case for Natural Law* (Grand Rapids: Acton Institute).

VAN TIL, C. (1946), 'Nature and Scripture', in N. B. Stonehouse and P. Woolley (eds.), *The Infallible Word: A Symposium* (Phillipsburg: P. & R.), 263–301.

— (1974), *An Introduction to Systematic Theology* (Phillipsburg: P. & R.).

WEAVER, J. D. (2001), *The Nonviolent Atonement* (Grand Rapids: Eerdmans).

— (2005), 'Jesus' Death and the Non-Violent Victory of God', in Barrow and Bartley (2005: 47–60).

WENHAM, J. (1993), *Christ and the Bible* (Guildford, Surrey: Eagle).

WILLIAMS, G. J. (2007), 'Penal Substitution: A Response to Recent Criticisms', *Journal of the Evangelical Theological Society* 50.1: 71–86.

— (2008), 'Karl Barth and the Doctrine of the Atonement', in D. Gibson and D. Strange (eds.), *Engaging with Karl Barth: Contemporary Evangelical Critiques* (Nottingham: Apollos), 232–272.

WILLIAMS, M. (1992), 'A Restorational Alternative to Augustinian Verticalist Eschatology', *Pro rege* (June): 11–24.

WOODHOUSE, J. (1988), 'Evangelism and Social Responsibility', in B. Webb (ed.), *Christians in Society* (Homebush West: Lancer), 3–26.

WRIGHT, C. J. H. (2005), 'The Ethical Authority of the Biblical Social Vision', in Schluter and Ashcroft (2005: 67–81).

ZIESLER, J. (1989), *Paul's Letter to the Romans* (London: SCM).